Advance Praise for

The Laszlo Chronicle

"Gyorgyi Szabo's book illuminates the work and writing of Ervin Laszlo—a renaissance man dedicated to a deep understanding of the nature of the universe and a hopeful path for the human journey. With discerning mastery, Szabo transforms the complexity of Laszlo's work into an engaging and accessible book that I highly recommend for anyone seeking to understand this pioneering author."

—Duane Elgin

Author of *The Living Universe, Awakening Earth, and Voluntary Simplicity*

"Ervin Laszlo is, arguably, our most visionary Thinker and Philosopher alive today and it has been my honour and privilege to have known him for over 30 years.

Gyorgyi Szabo makes an enormously useful contribution to the wider dissemination, the broader impact, of Ervin Laszlo's scholarship and wisdom. *The Laszlo Chronicle* could not be more timely at this present tragically turbulent time in the history of our glorious planet. I salute her!"

—Lady Montagu of Beaulieu

Palace House

Beaulieu

"The perennial quest in philosophy, as in physics, is for a unified field theory within which all data points can be synthesized into an integrated whole. It must be a system in which both matter and consciousness, history and eternity, ancient thought and modern science conjoin in a synthesis that ignites wonder at the extraordinary mystery in which we find ourselves. It must be a system that makes us feel grounded in all that is.

Gyorgyi Szabo has attempted such a quest. Working through a dazzling array of thinking from Whitehead, Bertalanffy, and Prigogine, and utilizing the majestic systems framework of Ervin Laszlo, she culminates her study with what is simultaneously the most ancient mystical understanding and the most audacious scientific speculation about what it is that unites all of cosmic reality, including humanity, into one seamless whole—the Akashic Field. In providing this synthesis, she has provided for all of us a holistic way of understanding ourselves and feeling at home in the universe. One becomes more human, more humble, more compassionate as a result of reading her work."

—Dr. Jim Garrison
President and Founder Ubiquity University

"Ervin Laszlo is one of the seminal evolutionary pioneers of our time. He has uncovered the science based, vital elements of how nature works to evolve to ever more complex and coherent systems so that we can apply this knowledge toward guiding our own conscious evolution. For the first time his work has been brilliantly synthesized and clarified by Gyorgyi Szabo in a scholarly yet profoundly interesting work. This is vital reading for all of us working toward the evolution of our world."

—Barbara Marx Hubbard
Foundation for Conscious Evolution

New Paradigm Books of
The Laszlo Institute of New Paradigm Research
Kingsley L. Dennis, Series Editor

What Is Consciousness? Three Sages Look Behind the Veil
(June 2016)

What Is Reality? The New Map of Cosmos and Consciousness
(October 2016)

The Laszlo Chronicle: A Global Thinker's Journey from Systems to Consciousness and the Akashic Field
(January 2017)

"Gyorgyi Szabo's work is a tour de force. We are immers
history of some of the most important scientific approa
developments through her thoughtful intellectual biog
Ervin Laszlo a pioneering thinker for over 50 years. Co
popular assumptions, Laszlo's most groundbreaking wo
now appearing, and Szabo leads the reader through th
plex, fascinating, and sometimes mind-boggling ideas
and grace."

—Alfonso Montu

Professor, California Institute of Integ

The Laszlo Chronicle

A Global Thinker's Journey from Systems to Consciousness and the Akashic Field

Gyorgyi Szabo, PhD

Foreword by Ervin Laszlo

A New Paradigm Book of
The Laszlo Institute of New Paradigm Research
Kingsley L. Dennis, Series Editor

SelectBooks, Inc.
New York

This edition published by SelectBooks, Inc.
For information address SelectBooks, Inc., New York, New York.

First Edition

ISBN 978-1-59079-396-1

Library of Congress Cataloging-in-Publication Data

Names: Szabo, Gyorgyi, author.
Title: The Laszlo chronicle : a global thinker's journey from systems to consciousness and the Akashic field / Dr. Gyorgyi Szabo ; foreword by Ervin Laszlo.
Description: First [edition]. | New York : SelectBooks, Inc., 2017. |
Series:
New paradigm books of the Laszlo Institute of New Paradigm Research |
Includes bibliographical references and index.
Identifiers: LCCN 2016020161 | ISBN 9781590793961 (hardbound book : alk. paper)
Subjects: LCSH: Akashic records. | Laszlo, Ervin, 1932-
Classification: LCC BF1045.A44 S93 2017 | DDC 199/.439--dc23 LC record available at https://lccn.loc.gov/2016020161

Book design by Janice Benight

Manufactured in the United States of America
10 9 8 7 6 5 4 3 2 1

Contents

Illustrations

(Courtesy of Ervin Laszlo)

Foreword

Gyorgyi Szabo's monumental review of fifty years of my thinking and writing is a mirror that helps me see who I am as a thinker and a writer. This is no ordinary mirror: It is a parabolic mirror. It includes not only the principal elements of my thinking and writing, but also their context and, above all, the connection between them. Surprisingly, it turned out to be a holographic mirror where every element not just reflects, but holds the seeds of the other elements that grew into the whole.

Never has the much-repeated saying "the whole is more than the sum of its parts" held such a clear and evident meaning for me as it does in this book. The narrative shows that unbeknown to, and certainly not consciously intended by me, my lifework in science and philosophy forms a structurally and dynamically evolving whole. The creation of that whole started with my ambitious (and rather presumptuous) attempt to rethink on my own the great metaphysical systems of the past and their relevance to life and society, and it continued with the discovery that the universal entity that evolves and becomes all things in the world is a system: a dynamic, interconnected, co-evolving system we call cell, organism, society, galaxy, and a myriad of other things.

The evolution of my thinking then lead to the realization that the rock-bottom, or better, the womb, of the universe and of the things that emerge and evolve in the universe, is an information field that physicists call the quantum vacuum and the ancient rishis knew as the Akasha. This prompted the further realization that we are all emergents in the Akasha, part of the Akasha, and one with each other through the Akasha. This is the quintessence of what I call the Akasha paradigm: the conceptual framework for guiding our thinking and acting so that it would reflect the nature of the world and our own nature as consciously evolving systems in the world.

The holographic mirror held up in this book by Gyorgyi tells me much about myself and the meaning of what I attempted to achieve in my life. It is my sincere hope that this will also provide insights to share with the reader—insights that go beyond revealing the features of one man's work—and throw light on the great questions of life and existence: who we are, what the world is, and what the essence and meaning of our role in the world becomes.

Ervin Laszlo
November 2016

Acknowledgments

Ervin, you have inspired me over the years, as you have inspired so many others. Your philosophical and scientific influence is vitally important for the continued evolution of humankind. It was my intention in this book to present your ideas, your passion, and your aspiration as a potential, and potentially powerful, driving force as our species faces the challenge not just to survive, but to create a sustainable and peaceful world where we can all live with respect for each other and for nature. I hope that my book faithfully mirrors what you wished to achieve. Thank you for being my mentor and my friend.

Anne Andrault played a crucial role in this endeavor. Not only has she translated my doctoral thesis (which serves as the backbone of this book from English to French in accordance with the requirement for a doctoral thesis at the Sorbonne), but she also carefully edited the text to make it mainly general rather than primarily academic. I can never thank her enough for her generosity in investing her time, expertise, and kindness in this project. Above all, she is a true and amazing friend to me.

I thank you very much dear Eric Franklin in Wales, who kindly adjusted the grammatical inconsistencies as well as offered changes for a better-read manuscript. Your amazing help was as valuable as it was unforgettable.

Dear Bill Gladstone, you are a great friend as well as an outstanding agent to Ervin and to me. Thank you for all your help, and for believing in this book. I am forever grateful to you for having introduced me to Kenzi Sugihara and SelectBooks. I will never forget my philosophical conversations with Kenzi about this book, and how we toasted in New York with a glass of French wine when we signed the contract to publish it. This was the launch of a precious collaboration between likeminded individuals dedicated to making this world a better place. Kenzi's lovely wife Nancy edited and polished the manuscript wonderfully. Her kindness and caring shone through the letters she addressed to me as much as in the work she has done as my in-house editor.

My heartfelt thanks go to my wonderful parents and lovely sister, and to my amazing friends Nathalie Barneix, Shauna MacDonald, and Scott Marshall Brandon, who have all put up with my obsession of researching and writing for endless hours, days, and months. Without their love and patience this book would have not become a living reality.

It is through the combined generous contributions of their time and effort of all these friends and colleagues that Ervin's lifetime of thought expressed in The Laszlo Chronicle has become accessible to readers everywhere. I am deeply grateful to them all, and herewith offer them my personal and most sincere appreciation.

Introduction

This study analyses fifty years of philosophical work by Ervin Laszlo. It observes the major turning points in the evolution of his thinking and looks into who influenced his progress and with what result.

Before turning to the findings of contemporary science, Laszlo began by studying the works of Plato and Aristotle. Plato said ". . . philosophy begins in wonder."* Laszlo's "wonder" meant not doubting or arguing against accepted beliefs but establishing satisfactory answers to his questions. In his view, philosophy lacked a factual basis and science appeared restrictive because of its compartmentalization into specialties. Laszlo's problem-solving approach commenced with studying the works of writers who have combined philosophical profundity with scientific acumen.

Alfred North Whitehead's[1] concept of "philosophy of organism" provided Laszlo with considerable answers to questions about the nature of the world and whether humans are more than just evanescent results of unexplored consciousness.

* Plato, *Theaetetus*, translated by Benjamin Jowett (Teddington, Middlesex: Echo Library, 2006), p.25.

Whitehead provided Laszlo with answers, but not the final answer. Laszlo then turned his attention to the work of Ludwig von Bertalanffy, a biologist and integrative philosopher. Working with von Bertalanffy, Laszlo developed the Whiteheadian *organic synthesis* into the *synthesis of a general systems theory*, which discusses a self-sustaining system persisting in a changing natural environment. Laszlo's pioneering work with von Bertalanffy provided a coherent fit with general systems theory and the findings of contemporary science.

Ilya Prigogine[2] re-conceptualized the physical sciences in a new theory of living systems in 1984 when he published *Order Out of Chaos* that aided Laszlo in subsequently creating a unique way to explain nature and thereby establish the *General Evolutionary Systems Theory published in 1996*, for which he is well known. This theory is centered around the notion of self-organization, which combined evolutionary and systems theories as the bridge between philosophy and the various scientific disciplines.

Laszlo's search for answers to questions such as man's relationship to nature and the cosmos, and the nature of underlying factors of evolution which connect all things, were not satisfied by working only on the basis of the General Evolutionary Systems Theory. Wittgenstein said, "In every serious philosophical question uncertainty extends to the very roots of the problem. We must always be prepared to learn something totally new." Laszlo did discover something entirely new—the theory of the information field—after immersing himself in a range of areas of study such as cosmology, consciousness studies, quantum physics, metaphysics and various Eastern traditions. The integration of his earlier works with his more recent studies lies behind his explanation of the existence of the Akashic Field.

The Akashic Field is a term that refers to an interactive universe communicating in a subtle manner and which connects everything with every other thing everywhere. This is a pure information field where communication takes place without the need for the transportation of physical energy; thus interaction can occur instantaneously regardless of distance and time. Coherence and consciousness are the bases of Laszlo's Akashic field. He proposed a "system theoretic paradigm," which focuses on a general understanding of the cosmos and the implications for entities such as human beings. This entails the observation and explanation of human and cosmic evolution as viewed in unity or inter-connectedness where macro and micro are essentially interlinked.

Laszlo's philosophical work extends to sociology when describing concurrent worldwide issues closely related to the existence of the Akashic Field. His humanist ideals are evidenced by his efforts to help humans understand the context and causes for their recent challenges and the possibilities that may lie ahead. Ervin Laszlo's half-century of exceptional philosophical work gives us the most coherent picture of the nature of the world to date.

PART ONE

The Discovery and Development of Laszlo's Systems Philosophy

CHAPTER 1

The Predecessors of the System Concept as Developed in Laszlo's Early Works

Laszlo' s first book entitled *Essential Society: An Ontological Reconstruction* was published in The Hague in 1963. In this work the author investigates the nature of general reality—"a venture of the interpretation of man, of his individual being as of his social existence—in the framework of the cosmic reality which is the foundation of his life."[3] He asserts that if one wants to comprehend human existence, one needs to understand the cosmos—understanding the macro in order to comprehend the micro, from the whole to the part. The object of his research in this book is the whole system, and his research method is holistic.

Essential Society is to be seen in this light: an ontology based on scientific findings. This is not armchair philosophy, but reasoned generalizations from findings, which apply to particular fields, and which can also be shown to apply to other fields. I highlight the importance of Laszlo's work in this context, especially because in the 1960s positivism was still in a dominant position in philosophy, and everything that could not be traced directly to sensory experience was branded metaphysical. Laszlo saw from the very beginning that science is not limited to sensory experience—that scientific theories explore the world beyond the limits of direct human experience and only test theories in reference to experience. This is not to reduce all elements, laws, or postulates of the theories to experienced "sense-data," but to test the consistency, the coherence, and the completeness of the theories as the most economical, complete, and meaningful explanation of the relevant facts and events in a given field of inquiry.

Laszlo originally wanted to entitle his essay "Essential Cosmos." Although he was very well known as a pianist, he was unknown as a writer and philosopher, so it was perceived as too ambitious to publish a complete worldview in a first book. Therefore he was advised to frame his ideas in the context of a sociological treatise that was both practically applicable and pragmatic.

Ontology, anthropology, and sociology give this synthesis its structural backbone, together with the analytical tools of epistemology, aesthetics, and politics. Laszlo repeatedly emphasizes that one can understand humanity only through understanding the cosmos and society because they are embedded within each other. The three sections of his treatise are equally important and are firmly interlinked. Ontology is the basis from which anthropology is derived in order to understand man, and to understand humans one needs to understand him or her as a being existing in society.

The publisher suggested starting Laszlo's discussion with ontology, because in his view the essence of Laszlo's essay is a cosmological ontology or ontological cosmology: one that claims humankind can only be explained by a general law. Since a pure, nominalist sociology does not provide a full comprehension of humanity, a general law cannot be formulated by examining human behavior. Therefore the general law must examine the whole system, which is the cosmos. In this whole system society appears, and in society humans appear.

In evolution, as explained by Laszlo, everything develops according to certain laws. Comprehending society, sociology cannot derive general statements from pure observation, it necessitates ascertaining the 'essential,' which is to be found in the laws of the cosmos.

Laszlo's evolutionary concept postulates that all that exists in the world, and all that *becomes*, evolves according to discoverable laws and regularities. Identifying and understanding the laws and rules of the cosmos are the basic preconditions for uncovering the 'essential' dynamics from which sociology is then able to formulate a comprehensive and coherent description of humans, society, and life in general. And it should be noted that at the time the book was written, positivism was a very influential school of thought, and concepts not underpinned by observations and laws derived from observations were considered "metaphysical."

He wrote *Essential Society* as a young thirty-year old thinker conversant in Greek and twentieth century philosophy. The construction and structuring of an ideal society in relation to the individual in terms of both parties' operational and functional demands are coherent, yet his claim to comprehending the cosmos as defined in his ontology in order to understand humans and society is not yet fully developed. What is the thing that evolves in the cosmos and also in society and in the human world? What drives evolution in society? Laszlo was searching for an overarching concept that would interlink and explain the relationship between macro and micro, cosmos and human. He found this concept in Alfred North Whitehead's idea of 'actual entity' and later in Ludwig von Bertalanffy's concept of 'system.'

CHAPTER 2

The Relevance of Alfred North Whitehead's Organic Metaphysics

Alfred North Whitehead (1861–1947) was a British mathematician and philosopher. He studied logic and the philosophy of science as well as physics, metaphysics, theology, and mathematics. The focus here will be on how Whitehead's metaphysical views affected Laszlo's philosophy.

Alfred North Whitehead's organic-metaphysical concept provided Laszlo with such a major impetus for his philosophical thinking that in 1972 Laszlo presented and successfully defended his thesis on Whitehead's philosophy at the Sorbonne, Paris, for which the university awarded him a State Doctorate. The Dutch publisher Martinus Nijhoff published Laszlo's thesis under the title "La Metaphysique de Whitehead" in the following year.

The basis of Whiteheadian thinking is that the whole cosmos is an organic unity of its elements, whereby organic connection links every actual entity with every other. An actual entity or actual occasion is what it is in virtue of its relation to all other actual entities co-evolving with everything else. Whitehead explains that in contrast an eternal object is not an actual entity—or an actual occasion! It is a Platonic concept, not a real 'thing' that gives things their individuality; it is not the thing itself because "each eternal object is an individual which, in its own peculiar fashion, is what it is."[4] This particular individuality is the individual essence of the object, and cannot be described otherwise than as being itself. Thus the individual essence is merely the eternal object considered as adding its own unique contribution to each actual occasion.

This unique contribution is identical for all such occasions in respect to the fact that the object in all modes of *ingression* is just its identical self. But it varies from one occasion to another in respect to the differences of its modes of ingression. Thus the metaphysical status of an eternal object is that of a possibility for an actuality. Every actual occasion is defined as to its character by how these possibilities are actualized for that occasion. Thus actualization is a selection among possibilities. More accurately, it is a selection issuing in a gradation of possibilities in respect to their realization in that 'occasion.'[5]

Whitehead's conclusion further explains that each object's relational essence rested upon systemic mutual relatedness. In other words, all eternal objects have the characteristic of the indeterminate relatedness of each eternal object as well as determinate relatedness to each particular occasion.

Laszlo never accepted the Whiteheadian thesis that eternal objects are unchanging. To him, they are also changing, evolving realities, 'ingressing' *in* and evolving *with* the actual entities or occasions.

Whitehead states that each entity can be united with all others, saying "that every item in its universe is involved in each concrescence. In other words, it belongs to the nature of a 'being" that it is a potential for every 'becoming.'"[6] This explanation provided a sound base for Laszlo to elaborate on the "inherent all-encompassing interconnectedness of the universe." At this stage of Laszlo's philosophical path, the concept of inter-relatedness within the universe was yet to be further defined. Whitehead's 'actual togetherness' denotes individual and particular characteristics affected *by* and *able to be* reproduced in *prehension*—the concrete facts of relatedness. The concept of *prehension* was a major influence on Laszlo's thinking. But for him, all actual reality was evolving in unison, including the eternal objects that 'ingress in that reality.'

Interrelatedness or nexus can be found in society, whose social order has taken the special form of personal order. The social order within the nexus denotes defining characteristics created by each member of the nexus. An event, here used in a more general sense, is a nexus of actual occasions interrelated in some determinate way. Laszlo understands that change within the event is the 'becoming' of actual occasions. The essence of actuality is that an 'eternal object' is defined by the characteristic of its essence which is eternal and elements within it are unchanging. 'Actual occasion' means the change of connections between elements, as they 'become.'

Whitehead defends dualism, in an interpretation that is entirely different from those of Descartes or Locke. "The universe is dual because, in the fullest sense, it is both transient and eternal. The universe is dual because each final actuality is both physical and mental. The universe is dual because each actuality requires abstract character. The universe is dual because each occasion unites its formal immediacy with objective otherness. The universe is *many* because it is wholly and completely to be analysed into many final actualities or, in Cartesian language, into many *res verae.* The Universe is *one*, because of the universal immanence. There is thus a dualism in this contrast between the unity and multiplicity. Throughout the universe there reign the union of opposites which is the ground of dualism."[7]

This definition points to Eastern philosophical tenets where yin and yang are antipoles that complete the whole. This is the Oneness as defined in Hinduism, Daoism, and Buddhism. Throughout decades of exploring and refining his own philosophy, Laszlo thus integrated Eastern views and the scientific premise of nonlocality to formulate his own theory of the universe.

The principal strands of Whitehead's influence on Laszlo's philosophy were:

- All things interact and make each thing what it is.

- All things evolve together.
- Things are not merely here and now—they are everywhere and at all times —the theory of nonlocality.
- Elements—there is nothing in the cosmos that does not co-evolve with all other things—there are no Platonic Forms or Ideas—what Whitehead called "eternal objects."

Laszlo didn't accept that eternal objects are eternally unchanging, i.e., that they remain the same forever, and he also never accepted the duality of the universe in the Whiteheadian sense. Laszlo stated that unity arises from the concrescence of actualities, not from the ingression of Platonic eternal objects. Having incorporated Whitehead's explanations, Laszlo kept searching for meaning. He found greater explanations of "meaning" in Ludwig von Bertalanffy's *General Systems Theory.*

CHAPTER 3

Laszlo's Discovery of Ludwig von Bertalanffy's General Systems Theory

The ideas expressed by Laszlo in his first book *Essential Society: An Ontological Reconstruction* (1963) and then his study of Alfred North Whitehead's philosophy were the beginning of his enquiry into what makes the world work and why. His second book *Beyond Skepticism and Realism* (1966) served as the next written milestone in his philosophical development. If evolution is a widespread, indeed a quasi-universal phenomenon in the world, then Laszlo wanted to know what regulated it and what was the binding factor and relationship between the entities that evolved, including those that constitute the world of life. He was first looking for a "noun" to describe evolution before inquiring into it as a verb.

The concepts of positivist logic and phenomenology helped to refine Laszlo's thought and provided answers to his questions at that time. In the fall of 1967, he was a resident Fellow in philosophy at Yale University, giving and attending seminars on a variety of topics ranging from Whiteheadian organic metaphysics to biology and cosmology. Northrop, one of the last and most eminent adherents of Whitehead, turned Laszlo's attention to the work of the Viennese biologist Ludwig von Bertalanffy,* indicating that the concept of system could be highly relevant to Laszlo's investigations.

BERTALANFFY'S GENERAL SYSTEM THEORY VS. LASZLO'S SYSTEM PHILOSOPHY

At the beginning of the 20th century, scientists and philosophers began to investigate the entities of the real world not just in terms of the nature of their parts but their *organizational* aspect as well. It became clear that complex things function and are structured as "systems" because of the relationship between their parts. Systemic concept provided the conceptual basis for describing different kinds of organizations ranging from the smallest organisms, societies, and cultures to the universe as a whole. Ludwig von Bertalanffy explains in *General System Theory*,[8] "It seems legitimate to ask for a theory not of systems of a more or less special kind, but of universal principles applying to systems in general. . . . irrespective of whether they are of physical, biological or sociological nature."[9]

* Karl Ludwig von Bertalanffy (1901–1972) is considered the founder of the systems approach known as General Systems Theory (GST). A theory that describes systems with interacting parts, this concept seeks to explain the works of "living things" in biology as well as cybernetics. Bertalanffy's mathematical model of an organism's growth over time is still relevant today.

Laszlo's *Introduction to Systems Philosophy: Toward a New Paradigm of Contemporary Thought*, published in 1972, was the first work using a series of paradigmatic concepts outlining the character of Nature, taken as a whole. These concepts are structured around GST, the logical ground for using them axiomatically being the evident order and intelligibility they brought to the understanding of Nature itself.

The structure of the book is built by grouping together Laszlo's principal ideas. The first three chapters present what he calls "The Idea of Systems Philosophy," and the last chapter states the metaphysical implications and the conclusions. These chapters are still read and admired and still prove inspiring to researchers and thinkers today. One of his timeless statements is as follows: "Man is not the centre of the universe, nor is the universe built in his image, but he is part of the overriding order which constitutes the universe."[10]

Laszlo states that "If the present attempt at outlining a general theory of systems, imperfect as it is, is any indication of what may be possible in more rigorous and informed theories, there are no grounds on which this kind of endeavor could be dismissed or refuted as unwarranted or invalid. The real world may well be generally ordered, and its ultimate modules or units may well be systems maintaining themselves in particular states of organization and evolving to states of higher organization. Moreover, such systems may be ubiquitous within that portion of the universe of which man is a part, and their joint presence could build the intricate structures which we have come to know as the complex and supremely balanced order of nature."[11]

Laszlo says that "Studies in Systems Philosophy" are really "Applied Systems Philosophy." They embrace ontology, philosophy of nature, consciousness and cognition, concepts of freedom and value, and they close with survival, a framework for a new age ethos: "I suggest that the role of consciousness in the syndrome of functions of human beings resides in their capacity to *learn*, i.e., to modify their cognitive and behavioral patterns on the basis of experience."[12]

Since all learning involves a phase of self-evaluation, it involves, for machines as well as for humans, what philosophers traditionally have called 'reflection' or 'reflective consciousness.' Laszlo says, "Reflective consciousness—the seemingly uniquely human capacity to know one's own states of mind—thus turns out to have a definite functional role in the evolution of learned behavior."[13] In today's language the evolution of humans requires the process of reflective consciousness—without which no growth is possible. This process has to be integrative in terms of respecting nature as an entity equal to humans. 'The use of nature for our egoistic ends had far-reaching consequences in altering the relationships which form the preconditions of our very being. These relationships took millions of years to evolve, and they could only evolve in balance, for any imbalance would have had to either be rectified, or result in disorganization.[14]

This is exactly what is happening now in the twenty-first century. Laszlo's words indicate that he had foreseen almost half a century ago what problems humans would face if they did not understand their place within the world as an "intelligibly organized system" and utilize their reflective consciousness. Laszlo claims, "Only man has upset the balance of his environment by favoring his own species over others, transgressing upon natural, and largely instinctual constraints on aggression, population increase, and environmental pollution."[15] One can hardly disagree with this statement. Then comes a final slap in humanity's face in his declaring that ". . . technological progress, the pride of mankind, appears as a tremendous blunder—an egoistical boomerang."[16]

PART TWO

Laszlo's Applications of the Systems Concept to World Order

CHAPTER 4

Systems Approach to World Order: Perspectives and Models

Laszlo's next step in his research focused on the relevance, impact, and applicability of general systems theory toward world order models. General systems theory served as the means by which the present state and the prospects of future development were put under a magnifying glass by Laszlo. The results of his observations and enquiries were developed further in four other books published within three years, as well as in his teaching as a professor at State University of New York at Geneseo, a New York State Public Honors College and in his role as organizer of symposia in the field of Systems Approach. This chapter reviews and discusses those four books as an important juncture in Laszlo's philosophical trajectory.

Systems Movement

Laszlo's creation of system philosophy serves as a connection between disciplines, neutral in the sense that research can be done independently without adhering to any specific school of thought. It integrates traditional philosophical notions such as ontology, ethics and epistemology with fresh concepts and newly emerging paradigms. In Laszlo's view, systems movement embodies "a new paradigm of contemporary scientific thought. It has unity through diversity, . . . an integrator of diverse fields of knowledge in diverse cultural and geographical locations. It is pursued on different levels, but with a remarkable consensus of basic commitments. And it provides possibly the most powerful tool we have today for effecting the unification of scientific knowledge, and the utilizations of that knowledge for humanistic ends."[17]

How does the systems point of view integrate diverse fields? In what ways does its organizational classification create patterns of world structure and development? What system laws govern growth and disintegration? Are there any specific equations that justify a belief that pure systems measures are possible at all, or that they are real in any sense? Systemic description of any field is formulated in accordance with its evolutionary trajectory. Influences such as forces acting upon a system internally and externally in contrast to its responses are what determine the outcome of changes. Science tends to explain external influences regarding functionality in terms of *what* these influences do, but not *how* they do it. Internal influences describe structural concepts regarding how a system does what it does without functional content.

Robert Rosen* suggested an approach to 'knowing' complex systems by way of simplifying them. This means that

* Robert Rosen (1934–1998) was an American theoretical biologist. His research focused on the most fundamental aspects of biology in terms of Complex Systems Biology and the theoretical foundations of living organisms.

breaking up complex systems into subsystems in order to describe them in isolation affords a way to describe the original system. However, this *modus operandi* provides only partial answers. What it doesn't address is the nature of the evolutionary forces that affect any system or subsystem's state or equations of motion. Evolutionary processes measured only by equations of motion within any system are not sufficient to describe world order models. Laszlo devoted great effort toward overcoming the difficulty by incorporating evolutionary concepts into the larger wholes that world order must involve.

Systems Approach—A New Perspective

Laszlo says another aspect of the relevance of the systemic approach can be seen in the advancement of psychiatry "that rests on the insight that the human being is an organized system, suspended in multiple systems, large and small, of physical, social, economic, and cultural type, and that his mental health depends upon the effectiveness of the system operations that govern his relationship with the larger systems in which he exists. William Gray* explains that the recent rise of the very effective methodologies of family and group therapy, which have brought many more illnesses into the realm of treatability, is another extension of the general systems idea into the field of psychiatry."[18]

The systems approach served as an essential tool to reveal the human being as an organic whole system as opposed to a

* William Gray is a practicing psychiatrist and the Editor of *General Systems Theory and Psychiatry* as well as the two-volume Festschrift for Ludwig von Bertalanffy, *Unity Through Diversity* (with Nicholas D. Rizzo Gordon and Breach, 1973).

machine-like creature acting as a robot. Psychiatry benefited immensely from such an approach, which gave rise to a new view of humanity as an entity in whom ethics, values, and symbols are integral and accepted parts. The broad theoretical framework offered by the systems approach provided the scientific base for further study as well as the possibility of including the social and behavioral sciences, which deal with human behavior. Von Bertalanffy's wrote, "general systems theory offers essentially a new 'paradigm', which is being elaborated. . . . and which can be applied to a 'new' class of phenomena. Concurrently the theories provide, 'meta-scientifically,' a new world outlook or philosophy."[19]

In his view, general systems theory is a kind of perspective that we humans can form for ourselves. It is a perspective that is not atomistic or mechanistic in conceptualization, but not a solution either in itself for overcoming all the problems of the individual and society. In *The Systems View of the World* (1972) Laszlo states that it is a perspective that does not look "at one thing at a time, and noting its behavior when exposed to one other thing, science now looks at a number of different and interacting things and notes their behavior *as a whole* under diverse influences."[20] The systems approach allows for shifting perspectives between hierarchies of systems. A subsystem such as a cell, or systems such as an organ, society, or the world, are considered as integrated whole systems with subsidiary components.

The classification or characterization of components differentiates by each respective system's substance. The systems approach observes the organization's elements, which give each structure its specific characteristics. Laszlo distinguishes two distinct basic characteristics: one, which is a non-varying, unchanging aspect, the invariance. The other consequently is the variant aspect. Are there any common variables between organic and inorganic systems? What are the shared characteristics between systems and their subsidiary components? The crux of this issue lies in its origin, nature, and role within the system itself. A human being is defined as a natural phenomenon of an organized complex system, in other words, a natural-system. A human being is a system sharing certain attributes with other systems. Specified criteria are applied to define what makes one man different from another or one of the components from another within any system. Criteria point not to the nature of substance itself but rather to *how* those substances are organized.

System Process and Progress

One feature of this organizational aspect describes how a system maintains itself and its relation to the environment. Laszlo refers here to the Second Law of Thermodynamics that states that a factor termed "entropy" can only increase in time in any isolated system. Disorganization is the result of such a process. It is interesting to note that the Law of Thermodynamics also explains that entropy may occur in such a way that subsidiary systems within the whole system can become more rather than less organized. Disorganization is the outcome unless certain external "inputs" reestablish order from decaying or internal reorganization takes place towards "homeostasis."* Laszlo elaborates on this point further as it is greatly relevant to the states and processes of world order as well as of the role of humans within the world.

A human being decays or, in other words, ages. He can repair certain parts of his body while tending toward total entropy, but regardless of the size of the readjustment, disintegration occurs. In Laszlo's opinion reproduction is to be seen as "super-repair": "Instead of replacing a damaged or worn-out part, they replace the entire organism. This way the individual organism undergoes the familiar life-cycle of birth, maturation, and death, but in its course reproduces itself and thus keeps the species going. The individual now becomes like the ripple on the surface of a larger wave in the sea: the individual, like the ripple is local and temporal, while the species, like the wave, is a vast and ongoing. Yet all the ripples together define the curvature of the wave itself."[21]

Change within any system is defined in terms of its system's evolution. The notion of preprogrammed progress, ability and self-creativity of evolution have long been questioned in connection with the concept and purpose of evolution. One cannot deny the fine-tuned coordination and connectedness between systems. Each system responds to another's states and changes as opposed to merely being passive. Evolution is a progressive development "toward order and integration, complexity and individuation, whatever forms it may choose for realization."[22] Laszlo explains further that "complexity of

* Homeostasis refers to a living organism. It is a state that regulates its internal environment and maintains its stability.

structure or function is not a goal of evolution; it is a result of it. There is no goal (or we know of none in our contemporary sciences), but there is a pattern all the same: the pattern of self-transforming natural systems in interaction."[23] Laszlo reminds us about the self-evident concept of the uniformity of nature as like conditions create like results everywhere in the universe.

Each system differs in its scope of adaptability and in its response to changes. Survival and extinction are determined by the extent of such ability. The success or failure of any social, economic or political system depends on its adaptive nature, compatibility with the dynamic nature of the whole system and external and internal forces such as:

- people's attitudes and worldviews
- dominant culture
- external threats by other systems (war, coercion)
- flexibility of foreign and domestic policy

Humans have a unique adaptability feature: consciousness. It allows planning actions as well as communicating and carrying them out in a purposeful way. It also allows for abstract thinking and the ability to symbolize. We can agree that in the past fifty thousand years, the human body has not changed significantly, but consciousness has. Consciousness is the product of long evolutionary development and is capable of change. Great adaptability to changes allowed humans not just to survive but also to dominate the world. At least that is what they believed. "Existence became social existence, within the context of a common set of meanings, communicated by means of a common language. Culture was born, and elaborate forms of social organization created. Man becomes a sociocultural animal,"[24] says Laszlo. Survival is encoded, but why did cultures evolve with such diversity? Could it be consciousness taking over man's evolution and decision-making in terms of what to create and in which direction to proceed?

Culture is bound to change and needs to keep on changing if humanity is to survive, warns Laszlo. Complex factors determine the outcome of a culture's evolutionary process. Above all, the concept of values ranks high in terms of influential capacity. "Cultures are, in the final analysis, value-guided systems. Insofar as they are independent of biological need fulfillment and the reproductive needs of the species, cultures satisfy not bodily needs, but values. Values define cultural man's need for rationality, meaningfulness in emotional experience, richness of imagination, and depth of faith."[25] What are values based on? In the early nineteen-seventies when Laszlo wrote this book, Western civilization portrayed a capitalist, supply-driven value system in opposition to a Marxist-oriented value system, which promulgated the elimination of private property and the division of labor and endemic nature of class hierarchies.

Looking back in history, we note that the development and progress of Western societies was predicated on advances in health care, the creation and exploitation of new technologies, the spoliation of the earth for the building of sky-scrapers, and the excavation of its resources to accommodate human energy requirements to improve our human condition of life. Human progress cannot continue to feature such a trend as it leads to disorganization of system, *the* system that comprises humans and planet. "Progress must be redefined, and that means a new system of values,"[26] Laszlo says. He proposes that positive, humanistic values take precedence above anything else.

This humanistic goal advocates individual fulfillment coherent with a multileveled society and in harmony with nature. Laszlo states that this is the only way for adaptive innovation to support the survival of humanity as a species. Humans are afforded the unique capacity for self-reflection—namely consciousness. 'To be a man is thus to have the almost unique opportunity of getting to know oneself and the world in which one lives. . . . Here is where the integrated natural philosophy of evolving sciences of our time becomes important."[27] In short, this is systems philosophy.

World System Models

The World System: Models, Norms, Variations edited by Ervin Laszlo and published in 1973, discusses world system models, highlighting those which do not work and offering new ones that may provide a tangible solution to the increasing problems that human society was facing at that time. Laszlo cited an example of nonworking world order model, the Forrester model that was coined and studied by the founder of System

Dynamics professor Jay W. Forrester,* Forrester used computer simulations to analyze social systems and predict the implications of different models. This method came to be called "system dynamics."

The Forrester model describes and predicts potential future outcomes for humanity by entering selected variables into a computer program, which in turn projects possible consequences. In Laszlo's view this computer-generated world-system model and its assumptions were not adequate to justify global implementation of its findings and projections. The model provides a globally homogeneous picture but fails to integrate local and specific variables such as social, political, and cultural factors. Without the incorporation of these factors, a world system model providing a one-size-fits-all model for global reform will fail. Laszlo emphasizes the importance of unbiased communication to people about the state of world they share.

But how can communication be unbiased? First, people need to have reached a certain level of societal awareness and to feel sufficiently concerned by the current state of the world model they share. The implementation of changes and systemic transition may originate from the bottom-up, spreading from an individual through communities and nations to a global scale. World-system modeling can offer a comprehensive forecast that includes warning signals and possible outcomes arising from either active reform or passive behavior.

* Jay W. Forrester (1918–) is a computer engineer and scientist. He is known as a founder of Systems Dynamics. He is the recipient of several honors in America and abroad. His numerous writings include Principles of Systems (Wright-Allen Press, 1968) and World Dynamics (Wright-Allen Press, 1971).

Mobilization is necessary to reorient current behavior towards active participation of individuals and communities in decision-making at all levels of socio-cultural organizations. How to mobilize people? As discussed earlier, changing one's consciousness can be the deciding factor. "[. . .] Laszlo believes that the growing seriousness of the main world-order problems—malnutrition and famine, recurrent warfare, environmental decay, crowding, resource shortages—will increasingly imprint itself upon the social consciousness of individuals and groups until even governments are forced to seek solutions," says Richard A. Falk* in his foreword for *A Strategy for the Future* (1974) written by Ervin Laszlo. Humans need strategies for their future. They need to participate actively and need not to expect solutions and actions by local or super-local governments; they need to act locally and embody systems world-order thinking and principles. Laszlo delivers this message more clearly in each successive book.

A desirable world order can be achieved by a form of strategy that "overcomes the instabilities and dangers associated with the current out-of-phase growth of material and societal technologies and their control capacities, and evolves the means whereby a high-quality pattern of life can be assured for the entire, still rapidly increasing human population."[28] Laszlo believes that people can and ought to do something individually for their own present and future and not leave the control of the future fully in the hands of governments.

---

* Richard A. Falk (1930–) is an American professor emeritus of international law at Princeton University. He is also an activist in world affairs. United Nations Human Rights has appointed him for several positions.

Concluding Remarks on Laszlo's Systems Approach to World Order: Perspectives and Models

With the concept of systems philosophy, Laszlo created a framework based on general systems theory in order to integrate information from various disciplines and perspectives. By means of systems philosophy he is able to outline what is incoherent in society and offer indications as to how to create a more coherent world order. System philosophy became his "language" through which he can explain world order to a certain degree. He observes and explains interconnectedness within the world without recourse to any religious or spiritual belief. System philosophy gives him sound understanding as to how the world works, although why it works the way it does is not answered. He briefly touches upon evolution and consciousness as the possible motivator for changes occurring in society and nature, but at this stage of his philosophical trajectory these concepts were not the focus of his attention.

Laszlo understood the urgency of inviting dedicated collaborators from around the world to start building a new consciousness that could help societies progress toward a more human and harmonious world. His ideas were put to the test through the assignment he received from the founders of the Club of Rome, to compile a major research study titled "Goals for Mankind." Laszlo undertook this study to provide a warning signal about the state of the world. It served other purposes as well, such as drawing attention to the use of systems concepts in seeking appropriate global solutions to global problems. To pursue this aim Laszlo then founded a new organization: the Club of Budapest, which is still active today.

CHAPTER 5

New Horizons for Humankind

In the of summer 1974, the Club of Rome* asked Ervin Laszlo to write a comprehensive report that would focus on the human elements and value theories that define individuals, cultures, and nations, and that identifies the ways these value theories contribute to current world states and new economic and political policies. The earlier communiqués of the Club of Rome, such as the analysis *Limits to Growth, Reshaping the International Order and Beyond the Age of Waste,* focused attention on the world's economical problems and on strategies that may solve them. The club recognized that it was important to enquire and define the goals of the human race towards establishing the well-being of humankind as a whole.

Laszlo served as the Project Director and assembled an international project team of individual researchers and research

* Club of Rome is an international think-tank that deals with current and wide ranging political and sociological issues. Aurelio Peccei and Alexander King founded the Club of Rome in 1968. It regroups past and current political leaders and aims to raise awareness of the crucial problems facing mankind while acting as a catalyst for change.

groups, academic and religious leaders, and business and government representatives to identify the goals and issues facing different nations, ideologies, religions, and regions. The study was published in 1977 under the title *Goals for Mankind: A Report to the Club of Rome on the New Horizons of Global Community.**

The systems approach provided the backbone for the report. It served as an important tool to observe and qualify the functions and roles of various groups, ideologies, and regions that constitute the world. The overall aim he established with his collaborators was that peoples and nations must cooperate to create a harmonious life for the benefit of all—in an imperative transformation from individualistic, self-centered, and short-term goals to a long-term, collectively inspired and motivated mankind-centered goal. What kind of common, global goals can be established that incorporate different cultures and races, age groups, and belief systems? This question is as relevant today as it was then in the late nineteen-seventies.

This project and the compilation of its final report provided Laszlo with a different an experience different from any before. In a certain sense it did not advance Laszlo's philosophical progress, but it was another important milestone in order to test that his ideas worked, not just theoretically, but empirically in the real world. His philosophical concepts to date were more than just theories; they were more than just highbrow ideas talked about around dinner tables. He proved that systems philosophy provides an intellectual framework capable of

* Ervin Laszlo et al., *Goals for Mankind: A Report to the Club of Rome on the New Horizons of Global Community* (1977) Dutton New York, USA.

explaining the world from various angles, ranging from value systems and cultural differences through political aspirations and religious beliefs.

His research over several decades, as discussed in previous chapters, allowed him to conceptualize a systems philosophy that proved him to be on the right track. The accumulation of his research findings was manifested in this project, through which he was able to demonstrate the validity of his ideas. For this reason, it is important to summarize this particular stage of his professional career, not just because it added a different element to his evolution toward the more coherent explanation of the world he was seeking to develop, but also because at the same time it aided humanity toward its evolution. The sad fact is that such outstanding work was not acted upon worldwide.

Overview of Goals

In the first section of the report, established values are questioned in relation to technological progress, international power states and changes, and shifts in wealth distribution worldwide. Many surveys had been conducted on issues such as world politics, energy, and food resources, but none so far had set overarching goals for societies or nations. "Yet the survey and assessment of contemporary goals is feasible, and it is of great importance, even though goals are value-sensitive and values are notoriously difficult to express with precision, and notwithstanding the political and practical difficulties of canvassing all societies and organizations whose goals are of international significance."[29] Laszlo emphasizes that first and foremost, the current goals of each organization, nation, religion, or region have to be transparent and known to each individual member.

Each section gives an overview of current economic, political, and geographical data as well as various national survey results. Each section analyzes a geographical grouping in a very pragmatic way without any judgments being expressed. Most countries feature a strong goal in terms of economic growth in accordance with their respective perceived national interests, coupled with dominant religious beliefs. An overall competitive trend is recognized that urges each country not to fall behind the development of leading nations. The advancement of technology and science and the increasingly growth-oriented nature of the West influenced all countries around the world. This was not just in terms of the West having to look for new markets, but because the concept of consumerism affected value-systems that were otherwise differently oriented.

Laszlo says that in the Middle East and North Africa, people "who in the past were accustomed to poverty and underdevelopment, and considered this an act of God, are now awakened and believe that their condition is not the result of God's will, but of the exploitation of their national wealth by the 'great powers' and the 'developed world.' This rise in expectations creates immense pressures on the governments for rapid reforms and an accelerated pace of development."[30]

The goals of international organizations such as the World Council of Churches,* the United Nations,† and multinational corporations are outlined, and these chapters close the first section of the report. The reader thus far is given an idea about the nature and diversity of goals and aspirations around the world. It is clearly shown that goals and expectations are changing. International organizations spring up to voice universal human rights and insist on the greater responsibility of nations, corporations, and social institutions.

Basic Assessment of Various Global Goals

The second part of the report discusses long-term goals and projects for a safer and more humane world. Long-term policies at local, national, regional, and corporate levels encompass issues of global security, food, energy, and resource goals. Laszlo calls attention to the concept of "outer limits" that affect human development. Humans depleting natural resources is counter-effective in as much as it slows growth and goes against man's long-term self-interest. Appropriate global goals can find solutions to problems such as environmental pollution, insufficient food production, and the mistreatment of our natural habitat. Such goals would produce greater justice, global security, safer and more abundant supply of natural energy, and the

* World Council of Churches is an international, inter-church organization founded in 1948. Most mainstream Christian churches are its members apart from the Roman Catholic Church.

† The United Nations is an international organization whose objectives include advocating and advancing human rights, economic development, health and education, and peacekeeping.

fulfillment of the needs and aspirations of individuals, nations, and regions.

World security needs to be addressed in such a way that global confrontations are eliminated. Military spending and nuclear armament is not a long-term option towards global peace. "But sooner or later the entire international community will have to join in supporting a collectively constituted and mandated disarmament supervisory and peacekeeping body. Unless collective reason prevails over collective madness, a collective catastrophe is certain to result."[31]

Food production is insufficient and food distribution inadequate. The application of new agricultural and economic practices could be generalized for safer food production, food storage, and greater justice in distribution. Reforming agricultural practices in conjunction with training would enhance global development while eliminating hunger in less-developed countries.

Wasteful and inefficient practices in energy use must be changed while developing new ways of utilizing abundant natural resources that are environmentally sustainable. Such goals are crucial to mankind's short- and long-term future. Laszlo says, "The basic requirement on world energy use can be clearly stated. It is to serve people. First and foremost, it is to place at the command of all people everywhere safe and clean energies that they can produce and control themselves. Energy must become the servant of people, not people the slaves and possibly the victims, of the available energies. The production of suitable energy must be sustained for into the future. The best-suited source of energy becomes inappropriate if its expected lifetime is short. The present generation would then be enjoying its fruits at the expense of generations to come."[32]

Any economic growth has to be considered in terms of *how* and for what *purpose*. For example, pure financial gain-oriented growth represses long-term human oriented development. Any development has to serve people, not any abstract idea. Food, shelter, and health are more important than material objects such as cars and luxury items. Any development has to be human oriented whilst environmentally sustainable. This entails global cooperation, responsible choices and appropriate strategies.

Relevance of Various Religions and Modern World Views

The last chapter of the report discusses how religions, ethics, worldviews, and ideologies need to focus their attention on transforming and overcoming the "inner limits" of mankind. Short-term, self-centered, and nation-centered goals have to be changed for the advent of a global community that would strive for human fulfillment with respect for nature. "Perspectives of thinking and action must be enlarged to take in the global and the long-term dimension. To this end the rapid growth of solidarity among different peoples and with coming generations is imperative,"[33] states Laszlo.

Religions and complex theologies constitute a major influence on humans. Their role is crucial in the formation of goals for humankind. Judaism, Christianity, Buddhism, Islam, Hinduism, Daoism, African traditions, and others affect the minds and behavior of the majority of the people. Their influence could promote the spread of humanism and solidarity or foster conflict and competition depending on the content of their teaching. Laszlo and his team suggest that the religions of the world have to overcome the divisiveness and exclusiveness and intolerance that marked the religious history of humanity.

It is noted that alternative cultures are emerging as a response to the current challenges of life. Dissatisfaction and fragmentation could be manifold. In general, these alternative cultures recognize the vulnerability of the Earth ecosystem and realize that human consciousness is obsessed with material growth as opposed to the consciousness of being one with nature. These cultures see no boundaries between races and belief systems, and they aim to achieve a responsible lifestyle.

Marxist-based communism, liberal democracy, and alternative cultures are all fundamentally concerned with human life and well-being, although they hold different views about how best to achieve harmonious living.

Inner Limits to Achieve Goals of Humankind

Humanity's growth lies not just in economic, social, cultural, and political development, but also in overcoming the obstacles caused by the "inner" limitations of people. The behavior of people and societies is considered a fundamental contributing factor to achieving any goal. This topic is discussed in Laszlo's book *The Inner Limits of Mankind: Heretical Reflections on Today's Values, Culture and Politics** published a year after his report on the Goals for Mankind.

Human activity is threatening nature and its own survival. In Laszlo's view, the inner limits of humankind are responsible for so much destruction that the recognition of the impact of its actions and the realization that betterment lies in the decision-making capacity of humanity is vital for action in attacking global problems. Individual aspirations and motivations affect people whether they are close to one another or unknown to each other. Personal behavior influences and impacts family, community, nation, region, and the whole of humanity.

What are the limits and constraints of human nature? It is evident to Laszlo that environmental degradation is not due to external inputs but rather to human action. Hence it is humanity's responsibility to change its behavior to rebalance environmental aspects for its own present and future. Is humanity evolved enough to recognize its wrong-doing? Does humanity have the level of understanding of the short- and long-term consequences of its own actions? Laszlo's book draws attention to these questions and reaffirms that "today we live in a truly crucial epoch. A merely four thousand days separate us from a turning point in the history of our species—a turning point that marks not only our passage to the third millennium AD, but also, and more importantly, to an age where we must take

* Laszlo, E., *The Inner Limits of Mankind: Heretical Reflections on Contemporary Values, Culture and Politics* (Oxford and New York: Pergamon Press, 1978).

our own evolution into our own hands. Undoubtedly, we have the knowledge and the power to do so. Whether we also have the wisdom to use our knowledge and our power to achieve this end remains yet to be seen."[34]

Laszlo spells out succinctly that humanity's self-centered, superior-to-nature, technology-dependent, materialistic, and growth-oriented for-profits-only behavior is counter-effective for long term overall sustainability. He doesn't question whether humanity *can* change; he questions whether humanity *will* and *when*, given the rapid pace of environmental destruction. Humanity needs not just *vision* but *positive vision* and adequate *revision* of human behavior. A livable environment is the basic for human life. Deforestation, overgrazing and overfishing, and emitting chemicals into the atmosphere through inadequate agricultural practices, can have an irreversible effect on nature. Human shortsighted views endanger lives.

Laszlo suggests creating and defining "a new international moral order" and a "new international code of conduct"[35] that would guide human aspirations and interrelationships. These would be based upon universal values that exist already in major religions and cultural traditions: universal brotherhood, love for one's neighbor and community, and treating others as one would like to be treated. The recognition of these spiritual truths is essential to rising above national and ideological divisions.

Cultural and political differences must be ironed out and new value-systems are required to change from a fragmented worldview to global solidarity and cooperation. Laszlo envisions that 'Through the birth of a spirit of world solidarity, the cooperative projects envisaged by the international community could be implemented. The world would change from an arena of marginal security and economic and political conflict, to a global society of undiminished diversity but firm collective self-reliance, greater security, and more equity."[36]

The "Inner Limits" is not a psychological study but rather an epistemological study on the nature of humanity. Laszlo observes that humans contemplate changing almost everything around them but themselves. He also emphasizes that one person's transformation is not enough. It is working together that creates global change.

Collaboration between international religious organizations, world governments, and world cultures is needed to accomplish the necessary change—together. The realization of the fundamental truth that lies at the core of the majority of religious traditions and philosophies points to the "oneness" of the entire human species. The failure to attain such a concept diminishes the chances of survival of the human race; it curbs progress and life in its entirety.

Laszlo's systems approach helped to construct two comprehensive studies on humanity. He observed the planet and the peoples within as complex open systems vulnerable to change both externally and internally. Components of complex systems become more complex because of changes by inherent connections. Human society follows similar functions as any other complex system. It evolves in the course of progress carried by an informational flow of exchange.

Goals for Mankind and *Inner Limits of Mankind* blend philosophical, sociological, and scientific concepts in an amalgamation that should have achieved greater worldwide recognition followed by action. These books are as applicable to our lives and the current state of our planet today as they were thirty-five years ago.

CHAPTER 6

Systems Evolution: *The Maturation of the Formulation of Systems Philosophy and the Concept of General Evolution Theory*

The Concept of Ilya Prigogine's Nonlinearly Bifurcating Dissipative Structure Theory

Laszlo was introduced to Ilya Prigogine's* comprehensive theory of change in the early nineteen-eighties, yet he only integrated Prigogine's work into his own constantly and rapidly forming philosophy toward the end of that decade. Prigogine argued and proved scientifically how and in what way. For example, he claimed the Newtonian model is still valid, although limited, and fits compatibly into a larger scientific image of reality. He claimed that old "universal laws" are not universal at all, but apply to certain regions of reality. Prigogine's discovery gave Laszlo extra leverage to expand on his systems theory and to provide a bridge between natural and social sciences.

* Ilya Romanovich Prigogine (1917–2003) is a chemist and Nobel Laureate; he is well known for his work on dissipative structures, complex systems, and irreversibility.

Ilya Prigogine and Isabelle Stengers summed up their theory in *Order Out of Chaos: Man's New Dialogue with Nature* (1984). They explained that there are two types of systems within the universe: open and closed systems, and these operate in different ways. Closed systems form only a small part of the universe and function like machines. Open systems exchange energy and matter—in other words, they exchange information with their environment. Social or biological systems are considered open systems and cannot be understood in mechanistic terms.

The Age of Machine focused on stability, order, uniformity, and equilibrium. Prigogine suggested that reality is more than that; it denotes change, disorder, and process. In his view, just like that of Bertalanffy and Laszlo, all systems contain subsystems, which are constantly "fluctuating." Single fluctuation or an amalgamation of them may result in a turning point that changes the preexisting organization irreversibly. This point is called a "bifurcation point." Its direction of change is hard to predict since the new formation of the organization may leap into disintegration—chaos, or into a new, more differentiated, higher level of "order" called "dissipative structure." Such structures are termed "dissipative" in comparison to simpler structures they replace; they require more energy or information to sustain them.

Distinction is made between "equilibrium" systems, "near-equilibrium," and systems that are "far-from-equilibrium." For instance, imagine a group of animals. If their birth- and death rates are equal, given sufficient external resources, i.e., food and weather, the size of the group remains stable. This group is in a state of equilibrium. If the birthrate augments, the state changes to "near-equilibrium." However, if the birthrate escalates rapidly, the system is then in a "far-from-equilibrium" state where nonlinear relationships rule. This system becomes over-sensitive to external inputs and reactive to even small influences that may result in a structure-breaking system reorganization. Prigogine's study of "far-from-equilibrium" states and nonlinear processes opened up vistas in order to apply hard sciences to explain social processes.

Order Out of Chaos: Man's New Dialogue with Nature sheds a different light on the Second Law of Thermodynamics.* According to Prigogine, the openness and spontaneity of processes give rise to higher levels of organization, such as dissipative structures. Entropy does not necessarily lead towards disorganization, but under certain circumstances it serves as trigger for and precursor of order. In other words, entropy may produce life itself. Consequently, due to entropy, certain systems may disintegrate, and others concurrently evolve and become more coherent and more complex.

The Integration of Ilya Prigogine's Nonlinearly Bifurcating Dissipative Structure Theory

Whitehead's cosmology intended to "define the conceptual field within which the problem of human experience and physical processes could be dealt with consistently and to determine

* *Second Law of Thermodynamics* claims that entropy of an isolated system never decreases because of such systems evolve randomly toward thermodynamic equilibrium—the state of maximum entropy.

the conditions under which the problem could be solved. What had to be done was to formulate the principles necessary to characterize all forms of existence, from that of stones to that of humans. It is precisely this universality that, in Whitehead's opinion, defines his enterprise as 'philosophy.' While each scientific theory selects and abstracts from the world's complexity a peculiar set of relations, philosophy cannot favor any particular region of human experience. Through conceptual experimentation it must construct a consistency that can accommodate all dimensions of experience, whether they belong to physics, physiology, psychology, biology, ethics, etc."[37]

Whitehead as well as Laszlo understood very well that the creative evolution of nature cannot rest upon permanent, unchanging components. Whitehead's purpose of philosophy "was to reconcile permanence and change, to conceive of things as processes, to demonstrate that becoming forms entities, individual identities that are born and die."[38] Prigogine and his colleagues investigated the physical aspects of change and permanence through their irreversible interaction. Their conclusion offered a tangible connection between science and philosophy.

The aim of Prigogine's theory was not to predict changes in a system in terms of interactions among particles or elements, but to predict how the system would react to external modifications. Laszlo applied this scientific reasoning to predict societal changes, and this became his focal message to draw attention to the current, and more to the point, foreseeable state of humanity unless some changes are implemented.

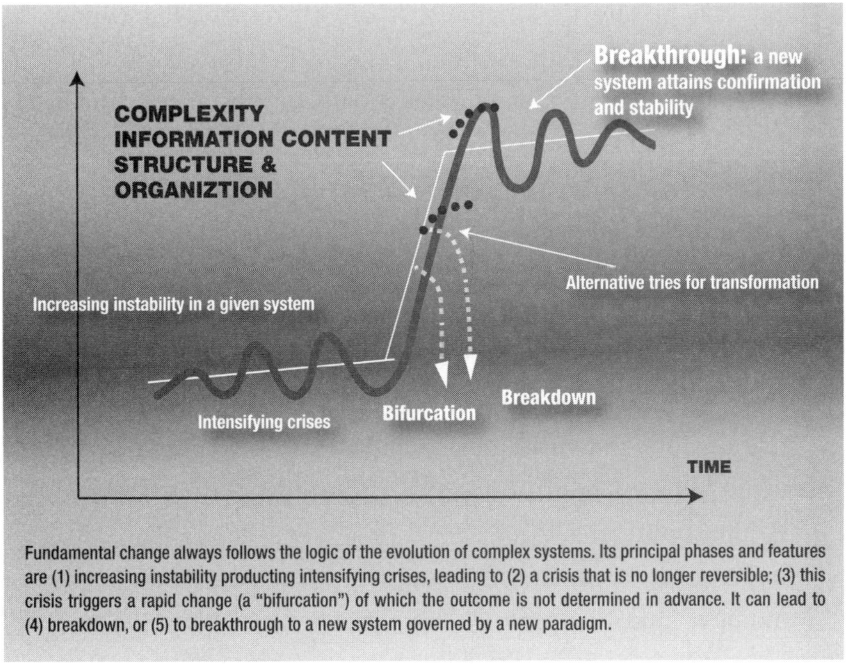

Bifurcations in Science and Society

(Courtesy of Ervin Laszlo)

Throughout his years of research, Laszlo was studying the causes and actual events of societal bifurcations and the nature of the succession of such bifurcations forming an irreversible evolution. In particular, Laszlo understood clearly Prigogine's scientific reasoning in terms of the outcomes of nonlinear processes in far-from-equilibrium systems. Such systems "may be described as organized not because they realizes a plan alien to elementary activities, or transcending them, but, on the contrary, because the amplification of a microscopic fluctuation occurring at the 'right moment' resulted in favoring one reaction path over a number of other equally possible paths. Under certain circumstances, therefore, the role played by individual behavior can be decisive. More generally, the 'overall' behavior cannot in general be taken as dominating in any way the elementary processes constituting it. Self-organizing processes in far-from-equilibrium conditions correspond to a delicate interplay between chance and necessity, between fluctuations and deterministic laws. We expect that near a bifurcation, fluctuations or random elements would play an important role, while between bifurcations the deterministic aspects would become dominant."[39]

This bears on the next question: What defines *the* 'right moment' and *the* favorable reaction in any system? To find an answer, the language of science and philosophy can be applied, while leaving aside any religious or belief systems for the moment. Laszlo suggested that a system's response to any fluctuation is not solely a mechanical reaction but rather has to do with the "information" element of flux itself. The information is encoded in nature governs all actions and interactions. Mainstream science considers this information exchange as obeying the laws of nature, Newtonian law, which was later superseded by the laws of relativity theory.

Laszlo claims that science does not yet comprehend fully the complete set of laws of nature, as it has not been able so far describe all phenomena in the universe. In his understanding, information in nature is exceedingly complex, and any complex system responds to encoded information. A complex system is considered by Laszlo an ensemble of varied parts that maintain itself in conjunction with its environment in a constant input output energy-information loop. This explanation corresponds with Prigogine's theory of dissipative systems. Laszlo views the universe as a highly coherent system encoded by complex information. Complex information is the basis of coherence in any systems. To maintain the integrity of societal systems, for example, stabilizing effects could be applied "where species and individuals interact in many different ways, diffusion and communication among various parts of the system are likely to be efficient. There is competition between stabilization through communication and instability through fluctuations. The outcome of that competition determines the threshold of stability."[40]

The flow and the rate of information exchange between macroscopic structures and microscopic events determine the direction of progress, which is evolution. The feedback loop of microscopic events influencing macroscopic structures can result in modifications of microscopic mechanisms. This explanation leads to an understanding of current and predictable future societal outcomes of human behavior, and it also provide a possible explanation on a universal scale. Prigogine said that without non-equilibrium conditions and irreversible processes connected to them, our universe would have acquired a different dimension from the one it currently has.

"We know now that societies are immensely complex systems involving a potentially enormous number of bifurcations exemplified by the variety of cultures that have evolved in the relatively short span of human history. We know that such systems are highly sensitive to fluctuations. This leads both to hope and a threat: hope since even small fluctuations may grow and change the overall structure. As a result, individual activity is not doomed to insignificance. On the other hand, this is also a threat, since in our universe the security of stable, permanent rules seems gone forever. We are living in a dangerous and uncertain world that inspires no blind confidence."[41]

General Evolution Theory

Laszlo integrated Prigogine's theory of non-equilibrium thermodynamics with its concept of bifurcation into his own philosophy stated in *Evolution: The Grand Synthesis.*[42] In this book he boldly attempted to achieve the unification of knowledge underpinned by a generalized concept of the process of evolution. His synthesis proposes that evolution is subject to general laws, which are compatible with and applicable to all systems. In Laszlo's view, evolution is an opportunity to be made use of; it is not deterministic. Its direction is unpredictable, but at the same time controllable.

In his view "a grand evolutionary synthesis can give us the large-scale map that shows us where we are in nature's scheme and that, like any good map, can allow us to identify the processes that concern us the most—those processes that decide the future of our societies, and thus of ourselves."[43]

At the time of the publication of this synthesis, forty years had passed since World War II, and the planet was experiencing a boom in population, technological growth, and political and cultural transformations coupled with advancement of globalization. The world seemed to be becoming even more complex, and there was a trend towards finding simple explanations for complex matters and events. Laszlo sought to find and define a simple, yet not simplistic, explanation for evolution that applies equally to cosmos, nature, and humanity. He wanted to relate the nature and progress of evolution between the macrocosmos and micro-cosmos in a way that would not imply a different kind of evolution. He proposed to identify "regularities and obtain a glimpse of the fundamental nature of evolution—of the evolution of the cosmos as a whole, including the living world and the world of human social history. To search out and systematically state these regularities is to engage in the creation of the 'grand synthesis' that unites physical, biological, and social evolution into a consistent framework with its own laws and logic."[44]

Laszlo looked at the logic of evolution. He noted that when strongly bound systems are exposed to each other, weaker forces attract more strongly bound components in order to create higher-level systems. For example, starting from hadrons to leptons, this led to quarks, atoms, molecules, cells, and so forth. He suggested that free energy-flux density—the measure of the free energy flowing through the system at any given time—was an important factor indicating the basic direction of evolution. It also matters how a system is able to collect, contain, and use its free-energy density. As the density of free energy in the system augments, it becomes more complex in structure. Thus evolution follows a "periodically indeterminate nonlinear transformation" defined by means of the following recurrences:

- destabilizations of systems far from equilibrium states
- influence of energy flow that pushes for bifurcation
- complexification of system structure occurring on each organizational level
- simplification of system structure for the next organizational level
- transforming weaker energies into stronger ones
- increase of highly developed control capacities to replace primitive forms of self-regulation

Laszlo's progressive transformation is triggered by energy flows, which result in a constant structuring and restructuring of systems. He asks, yet does not clarify, *how* a precise evolutionary trajectory forms and operates. He states that the appearance of the human species was not predetermined; it was the result of biological evolution, which "does not determine the course of its unfolding, but merely identifies the possibilities and sets the constraints. Notwithstanding the many specific features of the evolution of life, it shares its basic mechanism with all other forms of evolution."[45] Following his own explanation of progressive transformational stages in relation to bifurcation and the convergence of all dynamic systems, emerging species will be better equipped for their given milieu than their predecessors.

According to him, evolution is definitely not teleological; it does not imply a precise goal apart from its direction that originates from equilibrium and heads towards nonlinear life emergence. From such statements one can easily describe Laszlo as a nonreligious scientist philosopher. This description is valid at this stage of his philosophical voyage, but will slightly change as his research continues and evolves while he goes through his own "transformational re-structuring."

Laszlo claims that the laws that govern the evolution of natural systems also govern human societies. Societies evolve in accordance with other systems in the biosphere in a multilevel structure within the limits and possibilities, values, habits, and beliefs created by human beings. His evolutionary axioms are:

- The cycle of human birth, maturation, and death is similar to that of societies in terms of its processes.
- The social system's environment is both natural and social, existing in the biosphere as well as in the sociosphere.
- Society is not to be reduced to the sum of its parts' behavior and attributes. Particular functions evolve and special attributes acquire typical features such as self-organization.

- The ability to evolve alternative structures and organizational forms over time.
- A new organizational level creates a new system function that is initially a simplification rather than a complexification of the previous level's function.
- Society evolves through convergence towards higher organizational levels. Groups and villages converge into cultural or ethnic communities, which in turn may become integrated into provinces or states.

Laszlo deduces from the above that ". . . if we place the here outlined axioms in the context of a sufficiently large cross-section of historical development not only can we perceive basic patterns in history, but we can perceive that these patterns are consistent with the general direction and the dominant dynamics of the evolution of life in the biosphere-and likewise with the evolution of matter in the cosmos."[46] In his view, the evolution of human societies follows the governance applicable to systems in states that are far-from-equilibrium. These systems are prone to destabilization and bifurcation. Major disturbances, such as wars or technological revolutions, can destabilize the systems and replace the overall determinism of their functioning with intense indeterminism. In short, societies function according to the laws that govern complex dynamic systems in general.

Stable and unstable societies are differentiated according to their social and economic aspects, which define how their governance operates. An unstable society cannot safeguard the survival and reproduction of its people because of its depleted natural resources such as food or energy supplies.

Laszlo suggested that it is possible to select the most appropriate outcome of the forthcoming evolutionary bifurcations. But how do we know which outcome is favorable? The answer varies from society to society. However, in general, we can say that any transformation must favor long-term cooperation with neighbors and partners locally and globally as opposed to short-term self-centered economic and political gain. "The goals of social evolution must be broken down into separate tasks that can be realistically tackled by individuals. Scientists, humanists, administrators and ordinary citizens all have crucial roles to play in steering the next evolution of their society."[47]

The evolution of our societies and our species is in our hands, declares Laszlo. By understanding the system and becoming conscious of our own evolution we can consciously direct the outcome of our evolution. The exhaustion of natural resources and rapid population growth coupled with economic instability and unnecessary military expenditure all put a massive pressure on humanity, pushing it towards an irreversible bifurcation.

We can manage it only if we use our age-old wisdom to re-realize that humans are an organic and integral part of nature and reconnect with our natural environment. We must use our great technological advancements to favor instead of harming our environment and our species.

Evolution is not a blind, mechanical, and predetermined process because human beings have will and purpose and are active participants in their own evolution. Humanity has not yet reached the peak of its evolutionary trajectory. As conscious human beings we must act accordingly toward a conscious evolution.

According to Laszlo, "We are one of the most remarkable expressions of nature's thrust toward order, structure, and system, toward the hazardous realms of nonequilibrium where survival calls for sophistication and skill—and ultimately for mind and intelligence."[48]

Concluding Remarks on Laszlo's Systems Evolution

Evolution: The Grand Synthesis does not provide all the answers but it does offer a valuable insight that enhances our understanding of evolution in general. "We must remember, however, that it is not possible to test a grand evolutionary synthesis—or any conceptual scheme, for that matter—by comparing it with pristine reality. There is no immaculate perception: We do not see reality except through the spectacle of a theory. But not all spectacles allow coherent vision, not all theories, when applied to experience, can make sense of the strands of order that we intuitively believe interconnect the myriad phenomena we encounter around us. The best we can do is to prove the validity of our conceptual scheme by showing that, when we use it as a spectacle to view reality, reality appears coherent and meaningful."[49]

Laszlo realized that general aspects applicable to any systems at diverse levels of complexity are also applicable to the way systems develop. They range in terms of their complexity from atoms and molecules, to crystals and cells, to single-celled and then multicellular organisms, and they do so according to some basic processes that hold true as we ascend from one level to the next. These are the "invariances" in the evolution of the systems, and they appear in various "transformations." Transformations of the invariances could be understood like the shape of a circle is invariant with respect to all rotations, and a square is invariant with respect to rotations of 90 degrees. In this sense Laszlo's theory suggests that evolution remains invariant across its transformations and this theory is applicable to physical, biological, ecological, and social-cultural systems.

PART THREE

The Development of Unified Information Field Theory

CHAPTER 7

Laszlo's Systems Approach to Unification in Science

Having concluded the principal propositions of the General Evolution Theory, Laszlo turned his attention towards the observation and analysis of modern science at its turning point. Conventional scientific thought rests upon Newtonian laws of physics, the Darwinian theory of evolution, and mechanistic worldview, which are continuously challenged by a wide range of anomalies. In *The Creative Cosmos: A Unified Science of Matter, Life and Mind* (1993) Laszlo explores anomalies in the realms of quantum physics, biological evolution, and mind and consciousness, which leads him to develop the hypothesis of a *psi-field* that underlies and interconnects all matter in the universe. He investigates the probable nature and workings of this cosmic field by using current findings in leading-edge science while pushing the boundaries of metaphysics and the natural and social sciences, as well as reviving the debate between religion and science. Laszlo's conclusion denotes a creative cosmos that preserves and renews all that is and ever was, a proposition that offers the possibility of an emerging paradigm for an interdisciplinary science for the 21st century.

Creative Cosmos presents various concepts and anomalies, which undermine the pillars of conventional science. In this pursuit Laszlo unites the works of Einstein,* Bohm,† Dirac,‡ and Bell,§ while offering a plausible alternative: the existence of a psi-field. Now, at the turn of the twenty-first century, scientists are more at ease with the concept of "field," which has been overlooked in favor of the particular elements that compose it. Scientists had relatively quickly accepted four fields—gravitational, electromagnetic, the strong and weak nuclear forces. However, the postulated fifth field—what Laszlo calls the psi-field—was not so easily endorsed. Laszlo has attempted to bring more solid acknowledgment to this field by providing his own narrative.

Laszlo states that scientific inquiry has not so far produced any consistent single explanation with regard to the dynamics of natural orders. However scientific inquiry is steadily progressing towards such an aim through the development of

* Albert Einstein (1879–1955) developed the general relativity theory and the mass-energy equation of $E=mc^2$ and worked as well as on quantum theory.

† David Joseph Bohm (1917–1992) was an American theoretical physicist who contributed greatly to quantum theory, philosophy of the mind, and neuropsychology. He is famous for the development of the theory of the implicate and explicate order of the world.

‡ Paul Adrien Maurice Dirac (1902–1984) was an English theoretical physicist who made considerable contributions to the development of quantum mechanics and quantum electrodynamics.

§ John Stuart Bell (1928–1990) was a Northern Irish physicist. He is well known as the originator of the Bell theorem, a significant element in quantum physics regarding hidden variable theories.

cross-disciplinary concepts, methods, and theories that furnish an understanding of how things are *becoming* as opposed to what things *are*.

So how are we to decipher the meaning of order in the universe, and what is the meaning of its evolution? Acknowledging that the world is highly ordered, Laszlo's reply to this question is that order has to be the result of more than just mere chance. Supposing that "if a series of chance events had punctuated the developmental process, the things that would have emerged out of that process would have randomly diverged among themselves. Higher levels of order could not have grown out of such a set of randomly diverging lower-lever orders."[50]

Entities such as cells, atoms, humans, and ecology not only diverge in their evolutionary process, but they converge with and toward one another irrespective of space and time. What law rules these coordinations? Is it cosmic intelligence or nature? Laszlo answers that if whatever we see in nature is the result of evolutionary processes then it must be something that regulates evolution in the sense that those events are kept on their evolutionary path.

His hypothesis describes a universe in which all that occurs remains encoded in spacetime. "If the universe preserved and fed back the traces of its own evolution, 'in-forming' its parts consistently with the whole and the whole consistently with its parts, it could evolve towards order creatively and self-consistently, without either the mechanistic constraint of self-repetition, or the chaotic anarchy of unfettered randomness."[51] This explanation is far from dogmatism or any set of religious beliefs or even mysticism. It denotes clarity of vision and comprehension without any constraints.

Cosmological Revolution and the Unification of Physics

Science has gone through revolutions or paradigm shifts at various points in history. Belief systems about humanity and the world changed from prehistoric civilizations' myths and magic to ancient Greek rational explanations to modern age observations and experiments. The latter belief system dismissed classical civilizations' principles as expressed by Hermes Trismegistos's* dictum "As it is above, so it is below." The main concern of the modern age's belief system is material advancement and domination over nature.

Striving for a unified understanding and concept of the world has not ceased despite the spiritual hollowness of the twentieth century. There is a continuing quest to establish unified theories in physics, cosmology, mathematics, social sciences and related areas. The new revolution in science is pointing from a materialistic-reductionist concept of matter and mind toward a more encompassing whole-field concept. In Laszlo's understanding, such unification embraces all disciplines—it is transdisciplinary. The unification process will challenge not just one theory but every theory within any one circumscribed field of investigation, for "some of the most basic

* Hermes Trismegistus (birth and death dates are unknown) was a prophet and is believed to be the author of Herms Corpus, a series of sacred texts that serves as the basis of Hermeticism. He is associated with alchemy, astrology, and theurgy.

elements of our knowledge of the world are called into question: the nature of matter, the evolution of living species, the relationship between consciousness and cosmos, and the origins and destiny of the universe itself."[52]

Laszlo takes us through a brief history of attempts to understand and explain the nature of the experienced world. From the civilizations of antiquity to Napoleonic and modern times he reviews how cultures accounted for the nature of man and cosmos. He likens the Greeks' basic question to his own: How could order and diversity have arisen in the universe? Greek philosophy understands unity as "the One," meaning that "the One" is to be found in a grain of sand as well as in the totality of the universe. The macrocosm is in a feedback loop with the microcosm and unity is always present in the core of diversity. It is important to highlight these concepts, as they influenced Laszlo's thinking especially in the formulation of his subsequent crystalized concept of the Akashic paradigm, which we will discuss towards the end of this study.

The rise of the centuries-long mechanistic paradigm started to lose relevance around the end of the nineteenth century and continued to cede ground during the twentieth century, although it was underpinned by the discovery of the second law of thermodynamics. Many classical thermodynamicists believed in the ultimate heat-death of the cosmos, while evolutionary philosophers like Henri Bergson* suggested that a specific force called *élan vital* drives life. Paradigm shifts in

* Henri Bergson (1859–1941) French philosopher stated that immediate experience and intuition are more significant than rationalism and science for understanding reality.

science occurred at a rapid pace. Even Dalton's* theory of the indivisible atom was proven wrong within fifty years since atoms can be divided into even smaller particles. The theory that matter in the universe was built of indivisible atoms collapsed, and no other comprehensive theory took its place. Matter proved to be divisible; quantum and particle physicists claimed that matter had dematerialized. Subatomic particles were regarded simply as "phenomena," which left the bases of objective reality a void. "By the second half of this century the ontological basis of science became entirely opaque. Not only could scientists not identify the basic entities that would underlie the diversity of manifest phenomena; they even contested that such entities would exist in nature. Clearly, neither the Democritean atom nor the Newtonian mass-point could be recognized as the ultimate ground of physical reality."[53]

Einstein's relativity theory followed by the advent of the quantum theory lead scientists away from classical mechanistic thinking. Cybernetics and General Systems Theory by von Bertalanffy, non-equilibrium thermodynamics and nonlinear dynamics as developed by Prigogine, as well as theories of self-organization and chaos had advanced rapidly. These theories explain that the connection between parts and the whole system is intrinsic, whereas the Newtonian concept of a mechanical world denotes independent forces acting on discrete particles. However, the human and social sciences were not satisfied with these new theories; for them Newtonian formulas of

* John Dalton (1766–1844) English chemist and physicist best known for his development of modern atomic theory and his research into color blindness.

cause and effect were still useful. In Laszlo's view, a more holistic and systematic approach is emerging that describes a new cosmology of wholeness through which we can understand not only how things *are* but how things *came* to be in the world.

The formulation of Grand Unified Theories (GUTs) has been the quest of many scientists, theoreticians and philosophers for centuries, among them Galileo, Boltzmann, and Einstein, to name but a few. Today's GUTs and Super GUTs are based on the four universal fields of interaction. These theories are incomplete as they do not explain "how particles, atoms and molecules generate the varied phenomena of the world we experience. In a truly unified theory of the universe, the progressive build-up of ever more and integrated configurations of matter with ever more differentiated characteristics must be an intrinsic feature."[54] Laszlo states the challenge, which is "to create an empirically consistent and internally coherent theory that would rise toward the pinnacles of complexity and order in nature with better logic than either chance or speculative metaphysics can provide."[55]

Transdisciplinary Unification and Bohm's Implicate Order

Physical observations and explanations of the world do not account for the dynamics of processes of mind and consciousness or of other non-physical levels of order. Therefore, Laszlo suggests, transdisciplinary unification is essential to explain all the forms and dimensions of order that emerge in nature.

David Bohm* contributed greatly to quantum theory and the philosophy of mind. He advocated that the workings of the brain at a cellular level embraced the order of quantum physics. In his view, the Cartesian model of reality was shortsighted and did not provide sufficient answers to all emergence in the world. Bohm's theory intended to broaden and unify conflicting divisions in the social world by positing a transdisciplinary concept that underlies the manifest world of experience. He suggested that there are two levels of reality: one, which exposes itself in phenomena and the other, implicit to it. This latter order, which Bohm describes as "implicate," provides the basic description of the universe. The word "implicate" has its roots in a Latin word meaning to "fold inward."

In this implicate order, space and time are not the main factors determining the relationships between the different roles of the components. Instead, a totally different connection between components is possible from which humans construct ordinary notions of space and time as forms originating from this deeper order. Ordinary notions in Bohm's explanation are called the "explicate" or unfolded order, which in fact have a special and distinguished form incorporated in the entirety of the implicate order. In Laszlo's words, "Because all things are given together in the implicate order, there are no longer any chance events in nature; everything that happens in the explicate order is the expression of order in the order of the implicate realm. Nothing new or random can emerge on the level of manifest

* David Joseph Bohm (1917–1992) was an American theoretical physicist who contributed with his ideas to quantum theory, philosophy of mind, and neuropsychology.

phenomena; evolution must be but appearance. Quarks as well as galaxies, the same as organisms and atoms, are once and for all part of the order that subtends the observed phenomena."[56]

Bohm gives primacy to the undivided whole. The implicate order is integrally part of the whole rather than just a part of the whole like particles and quanta. For Bohm it is the whole that is fundamental. It encompasses all emergences, be they matter, processes, or abstract entities. Nothing is fundamentally separate or independent in the world.

Laszlo accepted Bohm's implicate-explicate concept in his own emerging philosophy, but he did not agree with one aspect of Bohm's theory: the role of evolution. "Bohm's two-layered universe does not evolve: it subsists. Everything that comes to be in the explicit order is already given in the implicate order. Yet the origins of this order are not explained: the implicate order of the holofield* is merely postulated. Given that Q, the quantum potential, originates in the implicate order, it appears that the vital classical component in the quantum universe is to be accepted on faith alone. Its origins are explained neither in theory, nor by any possible empirical means—observation and experiment, after all, can only refer to the explicate order."[57]

Laszlo does not take anything on faith. He is in agreement with Bohm that there exists an order, which Bohm called "implicate order" and that Laszlo at first called the "psi-field" and later the "Akashic field." This order or field has primacy over all its component parts; they are all are enfolded in it. But,

* Holofield is the display area generated by hologram projection.

in Laszlo's understanding, evolution plays a dominant, if not the most important role in the processes of systems.

Ilya Prigogine's work on non-equilibrium systems is detailed in a subchapter as a contributory element for transdisciplinary unification, which was undertaken most notably by Rupert Sheldrake. An English plant-biologist (1941–) Sheldrake suggests that "morphic resonance" accounts for all forms and structures found in nature. Morphic resonance is embedded in morphogenetic fields that is to say form-generating fields. "Sheldrake's concept of morphic resonance explains how consistent order can arise in nature. This is a major accomplishment, rectifying the factor of randomness that plagues the interactive dynamics described by Prigogine."[58]

Thus far, all General Unification Theories (GUTs) account for evolution only as a chance occurrence, or as a past occurrence that recurs in the present without establishing itself as a genuine innovation. This does not convincingly explain the progressive structuration of matter in space and time. Their theories account for progressive divergence but not for the process of convergence. There is a missing factor "in current attempts to create unified theories of the observable and inferentially knowable universe. This factor is a sound interactive dynamics, capable of accounting for the progressive if non-liner emergence of diverse yet consistent order in nature. This dynamics is not likely to be a deterministic process, derivable from causal interactions among individual atoms or mass points. It is more likely to be a systemic progress, governed by laws that apply to entire ensembles; laws that create systemic processes that are frequently probabilistic, but never entirely random."[59]

Undiscovered Domains of Mind and Consciousness and the Missing Factor

Classical science claims, without offering tangible proof, that mind and consciousness reside in and are performed by the brain. No scientific theory has thus far been able to decode the entire workings of the brain. Human experience, intuition, inspiration, extrasensory perception, and long-term memory are not explained by contemporary brain or neurophysiological theories. Laszlo dedicated a subchapter to a discussion on the plausibility of extrasensory perception—detailing research results in remote viewing, telepathic transmission, and distance healing. He suggests that the missing factor in GUTs is the same as in theories of mind and consciousness: they fail to provide a meaningful explanation of the processes for emergence in the world.

What is this missing factor Laszlo is looking for? In the physical universe the transmission of information among particles is perfectly coordinated even if the particles are separated in space and time. In the living world randomness is not prevalent in the evolutionary process, as randomness does not account for order and consistency. Humans may be capable of transmitting information regardless of separation in space and time. All these, in Laszlo's view, call for a transdisciplinary concept, which does not necessarily point to an omnipotent Creator or to a limited scientific concept.

What is the linking element permitting information transmission and space-time connection? Laszlo answers that the simplest and most logical explanation is that of a field with particular space and time binding properties. Memory is an important concept. If one event is linked to another over time, the former is in some way recalled by the latter. Memory can exist independently of mind and consciousness, as shown by Rupert Sheldrake's morphic resonance researches. Memory is a vital factor in a hologram.* Holography enables three-dimensional images to be created with a process involving the use of a laser, interference, diffraction, light, and recording apparatus. In a hologram the image changes as the position and orientation of the viewing system changes.

Holographic information-storage is closely connected to time and space binding properties. Every part of the hologram contains the whole of the entire image by way of preserving an enormous variety of wave interference patterns. In other words, if a holographic image is broken into pieces, each piece contains the entire image even if on a smaller scale. "These properties of holographic information storage suggest that space and time-binding in nature is likely to function as some variety of holographic process. Space-binding calls for the simultaneous availability of information at different spatial locations; and the

* Dennis Gabor (1900–1979) was a Hungarian born electrical engineer and physicist. He is well known for the discovery of holography for which he received a Nobel prize in 1971.

distributed nature of holographic information storage responds to this requirement. Time-binding, in turn, calls for the enduring conservation of a staggering amount of information, and the holographic process satisfies this requirement as well."[60]

A universal field with holographic properties would have a nearly infinite information-storage capacity. The encoded information within the holographic nature of the cosmos could co-evolve with the microscopic and macroscopic elements that furnish the observable universe. Laszlo decided to name this enlarged and cosmically extended holographic medium the "Ψ (psi)-field." This field encompasses all the geometric structures of spacetime, serves as an intelligence operating in the womb of nature, and creates communication between human brains and between human brains and the environment.

In Laszlo's view the Ψ (psi)-field could be the missing factor in transdisciplinary unification. To him the "Ψ (psi)-effect is manifest not only in the evolution of the matter-energy systems, but also in the evolution of the physical parameters that are the precondition of this evolution."[61] Laszlo's Ψ (psi)-field is a temporally infinite, spatially finite, self-renewing and interacting system that constantly adapts to the evolution of complexity and thus to the evolution of life.

Laszlo refers to the Eastern philosophical and spiritual traditions of China, India and Greece. He lists the five principal states of the manifest world according to Indian belief: matter (Prithvi, water (Jal), fire (Agni), air (Vayu), and ether Akash (or Akasha) as the primal state. Akasha is the beginning and the end of all things. Everything emerges from it and dissolves back in it, in a constant re-cycling process. The Akashic Record holds all that has ever happened or has ever been known. These records, act as a universal hologram or memory field from which we can retrieve information.

Concluding Remarks on Laszlo's "Creative Cosmos"

With this Ψ (psi)-field, Laszlo proposes a unified science that describes the behavior and evolution of all particles and any systems in spacetime. It accounts for the known anomalies. The Ψ (psi)-field is spectrally and holographically organized and is inferred from the observed fields. A unified science can help us to understand ourselves and create greater well-being by living more harmoniously with each other and the environment. Laszlo's *Creative Cosmos* denotes a unified interacting dynamics whereby our awareness of the "Ψ (psi)-field" contributes to the creation of a more meaningful and secure future. The *Creative Cosmos* presents an encyclopedic knowledge of the concise but in-depth history of science with its mysteries, anomalies, and cutting-edge research results and at the same time theorizes the concept of fifth field, Ψ (psi)-field as the missing factor that can bring about the unification of current theories.

CHAPTER 8

The First Formulation of the New Paradigm: The Theory of the Psi-Field and the Next State of the 5th Field

Fundamental changes affect all spheres of life in business, politics, society, health and well-being, ecology, economy, and science. The theories of science are themselves subject to change—they are not indefinitely tenable. Historians and sociologists of science understand that scientific knowledge progresses by the accumulation of scientific knowledge as well as through leaps from one fundamental theoretical conception to another. Leaps can be understood as scientific revolutions or scientific paradigm-shifts.

Changes in science are triggered by the new and unexpected, and initially unexplained observations. When the key observations fail to conform to the current dominant scientific theory, the theories must be revised, or they will break down. The turn of the twenty-first century is witnessing deepening anomalies in cosmology, physics, biology, and consciousness studies, which must lead at the very least to a profound revision of scientific theories, or even to the occurrence of a scientific leap. Regardless of the nature or speed of the forthcoming scientific revolution, its outcome will point towards an integral science that will give humanity a more complete explanation of a coherent universe where all things are interconnected in such a way that information is conveyed by an intrinsic energy field. This is the object and subject of Laszlo's book *The Connectivity Hypothesis: Foundations of an Integral Science of Quantum, Cosmos, Life and Consciousness* published in 2003.

Laszlo explains that new evidence calls scientists to explain an "unsuspected" form and level of coherence in nature. He says, "This kind of coherence means a quasi-instantaneously synchronized state, with nonconventional connections between the parts that make up a system, and between the systems and their environment. Such connections seem to obtain over all finite distances and finite times, and they suggest that the 'nonlocality' discovered in the microscopic domain of the quantum may extend into the macroscopic domains of life, mind and cosmos. Nature, it appears, is made up as a nested hierarchy of nonlocally connected coherent systems.

"Time- and space-invariant coherence in diverse domains of observation and experiment calls for fundamentally new assumptions about the nature of reality. This book presents a hypothesis that responds to the findings. It suggests that space is not a vacuum but a plenum, and information, as physically effective 'in-formation,' is as fundamental as energy, and it is likewise conserved. These concepts serve as a foundation for 'integral quantum science,' a transdisciplinary unified theory that furnishes the essential element of the paradigm that will ground science in the twenty-first century."[62]

In *The Connectivity Hypothesis*, Laszlo weaves together the latest findings of quantum mechanics, cosmology, neuroscience, and consciousness studies with a deep expert knowledge of systems theory and offers an explanation to reconcile existing anomalies by presenting an integral worldview based on the sub-quantum dimension he calls the "Psi-field."

Coherence in Nature and Mind

In the first part of the book, Laszlo presents evidence of anomalous forms of coherence characterized as instantaneous and distance-independent coherence between all parts of a system. These forms of coherence emerge in diverse areas such as quantum physics, physical cosmology, the biophysics of organism, evolutionary biology, and consciousness research. Laszlo claims that these phenomena point to system-wide connectivity in nature, and such connectivity suggests the presence of an interconnected field. The concept of fields has been demonstrated in various disciplines. Laszlo suggests that the overall consistency of nature presupposes the possibility of a fundamental field that fosters specific physical, biological, and transpersonal effects. This field is responsible for executing similar but locally differentiated effects at different scales of size and complexity in systems composed of different elements.

Coherence in the physical world can be investigated in the microscale as well as the macroscale domains. Microscale or quantum-scale coherence applies to the nature and behavior of quanta. The state of the quantum is mapped by a particular wave function that encompasses all the potential states the quantum can manifest. It possesses both wave and corpuscle properties. Measurement and observation collapses the wave function into a deterministic state. What is in the observation that determines which state quanta occupy? It is believed that the consciousness of the observer interacts with the particle. However, experiments confirm that the collapse of the wave function may also come about in the absence of a conscious observer. Measurements of a particle's locus and dynamics has attracted as much thinking and experimentation as the role of a conscious observer.

Heisenberg's* uncertainty principle states that a particle's position and motion cannot be determined or measured simultaneously. This theory was challenged by the team of Einstein-Podolski†-Rosen‡ in 1935. Their thought-experiment split a particle in two halves and separated them in space. It then measured one half in order to ascertain whether this has an effect on the state of the other. It does and it turns out that particle A "knows" when particle B is measured. A does not only reveal B's state but actively produces such a state.

---

* Werner Heisenberg (1901–1976) was a German theoretical physicist and one of the key creators of quantum mechanics.

† Boris Podolski (1896–1966) was an American physicist.

‡ Nathan Rosen (1909–1995) was an American physicist.

Empirical experiments aiming to prove nonlocal connection between particles were carried out by Alain Aspect* and his team in 1980. Their work provided sufficient proof that particles separated in space and time "remain correlated as long as they had once assumed the same quantum state, that is, were part of the same coordinate system. The results can be extrapolated to show that the correlations between quanta are invariant in regard to distance and time. Quanta that at one time and one place occupied the same quantum state can be light years apart in space and thousands of years apart in time, and still remain correlated."[63] Laszlo notes that the nature of nonlocality and entanglement is not yet fully understood, but the existence of the phenomena suggests space- and time-transcending coherence among quanta.

Macro scale coherence was previously thought to belong to "classical" phenomena. In Laszlo's view, this is no longer the case. Anomalous forms of coherence can occur at macroscopic scales as well as at cosmic scales. The fine-tuned coherence of the universe seems to justify such claims. Universal constants and forces are so coherently tuned that they allowed the evolution of complex systems, including the emergence of life. The accidental probability of the occurrence of such macro-scale coherence is negligible. System-wide coherence applies to all scales be they quantum scale, cosmic scale, or living organisms scale. "Dynamic order in the organism is an order where the components are organized by a system-wide correlation that

* Alain Aspect (1947–) is a French physicist focusing on experimental work on quantum entanglement.

replaces randomness with a stable and dependable pattern. It is thanks to this correlation that organisms can maintain themselves in the inherently unstable and physically entirely improbable regime far from thermodynamic equilibrium—the dynamic regime required to store and mobilize the energy for life's irreversible processes."[64]

System-wide coherence also means coherence not just within any system but coherence in conjunction with its surrounding or milieu. In other words, living organisms need to be coherent within and without their own structure in order to survive and evolve. Anomalies also emerge in the domain of human interaction in terms of transpersonal coherence.

Branches of consciousness studies investigate the relationship between mind and brain to determine whether it is the brain that produces consciousness or whether they are two separate processes. Laszlo says that "quantum brain theory," the newest branch of consciousness research, builds models of the interaction of consciousness with the physical world, using concepts such as nonlocality, entanglement, phase-relations, hyperspace, and wave function.

"Despite great diversity of method and scope in contemporary consciousness research, most investigators agree that the phenomenon of mind is present both in the individual, and in the sphere of information and communication created by intercommunicating individuals. Mind and consciousness are both personal, and transpersonal."[65] Transpersonal contact applies not only between individuals but also between groups of individuals. The evidence for such claims can be found in archeological and historical records, such as the great similarity of Egyptian and pre-Colombian American pyramids with no evidence for communication between the two cultures.

Laszlo suggests the need for the revision of some fundamental assumptions of science to incorporate the latest findings and explain coherence between diverse domains of nature and mind. Transdisciplinary unification is essential in order to integrate the fine-tuned coherence of macro- and micro-scale phenomena and consciousness. His reasoning for such unification posits the following:

- anomalous coherence in a system denotes interaction among the elements of that particular system
- such interaction is system-wide
- system-wide interaction necessitates an interconnecting medium
- such a medium presupposes the existence of a system-wide field

Thus Laszlo concludes that "*anomalous coherence implies a system-wide field.*"[66] This system-wide field is not to be compared to "classical" fields such as gravitational or electromagnetic fields, and this field is not limited to the domain of theory. This fundamental field manifests physical, biological and transpersonal effects independent of time and space. To substantiate his claim for the existence of such field, Laszlo outlines the premises and postulates of his "connectivity hypothesis" in the second part of his book.

The Connectivity Hypothesis

Laszlo's premises for his connectivity hypothesis rest upon the finding that cosmic space is in fact a physically real plenum through which particles interact and that through such interaction the values of all the physical properties of nature are determined. The first premise discusses space as an energy-filled plenum. Space filled with energy was accepted in classical times by philosophers such as Aristotle who argued that the previously believed empty space or void is a medium conveying heat as well as light. Modern science acknowledges that space has both material and partly energy properties.

The second premise is that energies that fill space are virtual energies of the cosmic plenum. Vacuum or quantum vacuum was superseded by the acceptance of the cosmic plenum, which "is a virtual plasma, consisting of energy fields fluctuating around their zero baseline value. As the energy of these fields remains active even at absolute zero temperature, the energy that fills space came to be known as zero-point energy (ZPE)."[67]

The third premise is that the universal forces and constants of nature are in continuous interaction with the virtual energies of the cosmic plenum. Laszlo acknowledges that viewing the cosmic plenum as physically real is still speculative. Innovative particle and field physicists claim that this cosmic plenum interacts with system particles that make up the observable universe and such interaction regulates the mass of system particles, in addition to determining the universal forces and constants of nature.

Laszlo's connectivity hypothesis is based on his premises and takes them further in suggesting that interaction between the cosmic plenum and particles is responsible not only for determining the mass and the values of fundamental forces and constants, but for producing coherence among them.

The first postulate claims that the zero-point field in the cosmic plenum serves as a complex field containing scalar* potentials. It explains that "the scalar component of the cosmic plenum produces a physical effect on the motion of charged particles and systems of particles."[68] "Much as water fills the sea, the scalar field pervades space, and excitations propagate through that field at variable finite velocities."[69]

The second postulate states that information within the scalar component of the cosmic plenum presents itself as interference patterns that systematize the collective wavefunction (Ψ function) of charged particles and systems of particles. Laszlo notes that the quantum state is defined by the Ψ function, which indicates all the possible states a particle can manifest in space and time. Thus this Ψ function describes a domain of potentialities, which includes the unobservable and nonmanifest world of immediate interaction. In Laszlo's view, during the collapse of the wave function, which may be the

* Scalar is a combination of quantity like mass and speed that is completely specified by its magnitude.

result of interaction, events appear in the domain of actuality. For these reasons, Laszlo named the scalar field of the plenum "the Ψ field."

The third postulate suggests that the interference patterns that code the wave function of charged particles spread across the cosmic plenum indefinitely in time. "The coded regions of the cosmic plenum expand with the propagation of the perturbations. Ultimately the regions overlap and the wave functions carried by them superpose, creating higher-order wave functions. When all coded regions have met and their wave functions are superposed, the Ψ field carries the wave function of the universe."[70] Consequently the cosmic plenum must possess limitless storage capacity in order to retain enduring information coded by the wave functions.

The Hypothesis of (Quasi-Universal) Connectivity

Laszlo then presents the hypothesis based on these postulates that "the coherence-inducing response of the plenum to the presence of charged particles is scale-invariant and universal: It recurs at all levels of magnitude and affects all charged particles and systems of particles in space and time. This is consistent with the already cited finding in physics, cosmology, biology, and consciousness research. The anomalous forms of coherence obtain not only as nonlocality in the domain of quanta, but also obtain in the living world and in the universe at large."[71] He proposes that the integral wave function of the universe informs systems on all scales and sizes.

"In-formation," a term coined by David Bohm, signifies not only conventional energy but also the more subtle scalars that affect phase only. Information is created without the transfer of manifest energy, it in-forms the system that receives it. Laszlo says, "The in-formation of system and particles is the result of a two-way process. In one direction charged particles and systems of particles structure the plenum in their region, creating interference-patterns that code their wave function. In the other direction, the structured plenum—the Ψ field—in-forms the particles and systems of particles that structure it .

$$S_n{}^{\text{structuring}\rightarrow\hookleftarrow} \text{ in-forming } \Psi \text{ field}$$

The two-way interaction between systems and the plenum is not a zero-sum exchange of the same information cycling back and forth, for the wave function encoded in the Ψ field is that of the *collective* state of the entities that created it. It is never the single particle or the single property of a particle on which the wave function carries information, but the collective state of the system in which the particles participate; the wave function corresponds to the superposition of the state of all the particles within a coordinate system."[72] Laszlo's clearly defined information exchange explains that particles interact by wave function within systems coordinates. Their correlation suggests a high degree of entanglement. This correlation applies to all macro- and micro-scale systems of organisms in nature such as social and ecological systems. The nature of correlation allows for the creation of coherence-producing effects within any system. In turn, coherence suggests correlation in an interconnecting field.

In Laszlo's view, the connectivity hypothesis serves as the best candidate for an integral quantum science, since it presents the simplest consistent explanation of coherence in nature. This hypothesis regards the cosmic plenum as a universal dynamic background for all possible interactions including the transmission of information and interaction in living organisms.

Laszlo states, "On the human level the information conveyed through the Ψ field acquires a psychological dimension. The individual's brain is in-formed with the collective wave function of the human species as well as with the wave function of the socio-ecological system in which the individual participates. In modern people this information is repressed from waking consciousness, but remains present in the subconscious domains of the mind. Transpersonal intuitions and images together with species-wide 'archetypes' and archetypal elements are present in the psyche of all normal individuals. They shape emotional and intuitive aspects of behavior and may surface to conscious awareness in meditative and other altered states. The cerebral activity of generation after generation of individuals, integrated in the collective wave function of the species, in-forms the brain and nervous system of successive generations of individuals."[73]

Laszlo envisages a paradigm shift in science. Advanced unified and grand-unified theories are theories of physics to explain physical things. A paradigm shift is essential to incorporate physical, biological, and psychological 'things.' A new integral science will embrace all these in conjunction with cosmology and consciousness research. The foundation of this new science rested on *fields* and *information*. Laszlo's cosmic plenum is the basis of the entire realm of manifest phenomena that includes mass, energy, and information. The Connectivity Hypothesis goes further than the mainstream sciences of the twentieth century. "Integral quantum science will recognize that information not only defines the form taken by the laws of nature, but is a physical factor that connects phenomena and informs their behavior. Information in this sense is 'in-formation': the nonenergetic 'formation' of the recipient by the message."[74]

A paradigm shift occurred when Newton introduced classical mechanics. Then the next big scientific shift was provided by Einstein's general relativity theory, which interlinked the universe by signals propagating through geometric structures of space and time. The Connectivity Hypothesis proposes to shift current science towards an integral quantum science, which introduces a coherent universe where all things are intrinsically interconnected in the fundamental virtual-energy field referred to by Laszlo as the Ψ field.

Laszlo explains the course and function of evolution in the cosmic plenum. He says that "The overall process of evolution in the cosmos can be described in reference to the two fundamental elements: energy and information. In the manifest domain energy is conserved, transformed, and in each local universe becomes progressively unavailable. However, it is recycled in each new cycle of the metaverse. In the virtual domain, which is common to all local universes, information is created and conserved, and it in-forms the manifest domain of each local universe. As a result local universes become both more entropic and more in-formed, and the metaverse, energetically self-recycling, becomes progressively more in-formed."[75]

Laszlo's scientific observation and explanation of information exchange within the cosmic plenum is also reflected in his explanation of human and societal functions. The Connectivity Hypothesis sheds fresh light on the far- reaching potential of human interaction and communication. In his view, the human brain is a highly evolved entity with the capacity to receive sensory signals from the manifest as well as from the virtual domains. This understanding of human potential coupled with a new understanding of nature and the cosmos as described in Connectivity Hypothesis provides a fertile ground for science's next paradigm shift.

THE NEXT STAGE: THE 5TH FIELD AND QVT

Why does Laszlo consider the fifth field, his "quasi-total" vision including QVT that stands for "quantum-vacuum interaction," only a "quasi' vision"? A total vision "would be overstepping the scope of science. A more modest (yet already incredibly ambitious) stance is fully warranted. This is first, because a truly total vision of the known world would include spiritual and metaphysical element, and these—intuitions of the divine, of soul, and of other transcendent realities—are not accessible to scientific scrutiny, either now or in the foreseeable future.

"And second, this is because the items of experience that are accessible to science form an open set. New items could always be added to it, much as quarks, black holes, and superconductors were added in the recent past. At any given time even the seemingly most complete scientific vision is only quasi-complete in regard to the vision that could emerge at a later time."[76]

For these reasons Laszlo has been working to find an explanation that provides a "quasi total" vision to encompass both the visible and invisible domains of the world. Such coherent explanation could integrate our knowledge of physical nature with that of consciousness.

To create a unified theory, science needs to overcome current paradoxes and establish coherence between various domains of existing scientific knowledge. Laszlo believes that it is possible to find a common resolution and create unification based on a general concept. The concept of *field* is basic to such an endeavor.

Interconnections observed in nature as well as in the world presuppose interconnecting mediums and these are known as fields. The effects of fields are observable, but the fields themselves are not. For example, the gravitational field attracts bodies proportionately to their mass, but the field itself is not observable. Nonclassical fields such as quantum fields do not determine the actual values of the mass of a body; they merely state the potential for the expression of such physical manifestation. What kind of field could exist that transmits information through space and time? Is it a classical or a non-classical field?

Four fields are recognized by classical science. Is there a fifth field that explains the paradoxes that science currently cannot explain? The existence of a subtle energy field could account for the anomalies. This field may not be a classical field; it could be a quantum field. It manifests subtle yet universal effects.

In 1996, Laszlo called this fifth field a *holofield*, which could adequately explain the current anomalies as well as provide the necessary metaphysical concepts. It would explain universal interconnectedness, which is the precondition for creating a scientific theory with the quasi-total vision of which he speaks.

CHAPTER 9

The Development of the Mature Concept of the New Paradigm: The Akasha Paradigm in Science and Philosophy

Science and the Akashic Field: An Integral Theory of Everything (2004) is a result of Laszlo's four decades of searching for meaning through science and philosophy. The underpinning factor of Laszlo's TOE is *information* as a real, effective, and inherent characteristic of the universe. In short, Laszlo's Akashic field is an interconnecting, information-conveying, and conserving cosmic field. He presents a unifying world concept that explains the origins and essential elements of the universe: how and why it came to be as it is now, and how and why it affects human life on this planet. Eastern traditions as well as mystics and sages claimed the existence of an interconnecting cosmic field known as the Akashic Record. Modern science's zero-point field that underlies space itself is equivalent to the Akashic field, which in Laszlo's view encompasses the entire web of life and informs all living things, including consciousness. This zero-point Akashic field is a subtle sea of fluctuating energies from which all things originate: atoms and galaxies, living beings and consciousness. The Akashic field's other characteristic is the enduring memory of the universe with infinite memory capacity.

Laszlo found the simplest possible explanation, which ties together all the diverse phenomena of the world, including the anomalous facts of nonlocality and coherence in nature, into an all-encompassing concept—the Akashic field. This Akashic field provides answers to questions that have puzzled him for many decades, such as:

- What is the fundamental nature of the world?
- What is the essence of life?
- What is the world made out of?
- What is the direction and purpose of life?
- Is there a cosmic or divine intelligence?
- Why is the world as it is?
- Are there hidden dimensions in this universe?

Science and the Akashic Field proposes a bridge between science and the age-old intuition of the oneness of a cosmic plenum in an Integral Theory of Everything—the Akashic field.

The Next Paradigm Shift

Progress in science is marked by unexplained observations requiring refinement of the currently accepted theories. When refinement or stretching of established theories are not adequate to provide meaningful explanations for observations, scientists look for simpler and innovative theories that in turn bring about a *paradigm shift.* "The shift is driven by the accumulation of observations that do not fit the accepted theories and cannot be made to fit by the simple extension of those theories. The stage is set for a new and more adequate scientific paradigm, but that paradigm must first be discovered. There are stringent requirements for any new paradigm. A theory based on it must enable scientists to explain all the findings covered by the previous theory, and must also explain the anomalous observations. It must integrate all the relevant facts in a simpler yet more encompassing and powerful concept."[77]

Laszlo predicts another paradigm shift as the next necessary progressive step because "in the first decade of the twentieth century, science underwent a basic 'paradigm shift.' Now, in the first decade of the twenty-first century, puzzles and anomalies are accumulating again in many disciplines, and science faces another paradigm shift, very likely just as fundamental as the revolution that shifted science from the mechanistic world of Newton to the relativistic universe of Einstein."[78]

Radical theories and ideas, which Laszlo calls "fables," address these anomalies differently from mainstream scientific theories. Often fables provide an alternative, a more logical, simple, and plausible explanation of a given anomaly than established theories. Fables may eventually become scientifically accepted and valid theories as did Darwin's concept that all living species originated from common ancestors, or fables may fail through a lack of rigorous reasoning. Laszlo emphasizes that this growing number of anomalous phenomena requires cutting-edge scientists and philosophers to be open-minded and to reach beyond the confines of existing theories. In his view, these fables, which share the characteristic of *coherence* and *correlation,* are capable of becoming accepted scientific theory in the near future.

With regard to coherence, Laszlo underlines that "the kind of coherence discovered today is more complex and remarkable than the standard form, indicating a quasi-instant tuning together of the parts or element of a system, whether that system is an atom, an organism, or a galaxy. All parts of a system of such coherence are so correlated that what happens to one part also happens to the other parts. Investigators in a growing number of scientific fields are encountering this surprising form of coherence, and the correlation that underlies it. These phenomena crop up in disciplines as diverse as quantum physics, cosmology, evolutionary biology, and consciousness research and they point toward a previously unknown form and level of unity in nature. The discovery of this unity is at the core of the next paradigm shift in science. This is a remarkable development, for the new paradigm—as we shall see—offers the best-ever basis for creating the long sought but hitherto unachieved integral theory of everything."[79]

Laszlo gives an introductory overview of current puzzles in cosmology, considered to be a turbulent branch of the astronomical sciences. Cosmological anomalies share a common characteristic of coherence demonstrated by the following:

- The *"flatness" of the universe* explains that space-time is "flat" in the absence of matter.
- The *"missing mass"* of the universe provides for an additional gravitational force besides that created by visible mass only. Mainstream science considers matter to have mass in order to produce the force of gravitation. Even taking into account the gravitational pull of invisible, that is "dark" matter, we have to postulate that a considerable amount of matter or mass is believed to be missing.
- The *continuous expansion of the cosmos* does not fit with mainstream theories, which believe that gravitational forces are supposed to halt the acceleration created by the Big Bang.
- The *coherence of some cosmic ratios* present in and between particles and forces throughout the universe.
- The *"horizon problem"* denotes that macrostructures in the universe evolve practically in a uniform manner throughout the cosmos, regardless of distance. According to relativity theory, light is the fastest signal; yet to cover great distances in the cosmos forces

other than light were required to act the signaling entity correlating a universal evolution.

- The *fine-tuned universal constants* allow for life to emerge and evolve.

To account for these puzzles, it is suggested that the answer could lie in the possibility that the universe could have been born in a prior "meta-verse." A metaverse may well be more fundamental and vaster than what current cosmology observes. Laszlo believes that the existence of the Metaverse "could have informed the birth and evolution of our universe, much as the genetic code of our parents informed the conception and growth of the embryo that grew into what we are today. The staggering coherence of our universe tells us that all its stars and galaxies are interconnected in some way. And the astonishing fine-tuning of the physical laws and constants of our universe suggests that at its birth our universe may have been connected with prior universes in a vaster, perhaps infinite Metaverse. Do we come across here the footprint of a cosmic 'Akashic Field' that conveyed the trace of a precursor universe to the birth of our universe—and has been connecting and correlating the stars and galaxies of this universe ever since?"[80]

Next, Laszlo posits an overview of the puzzles of quantum physics. He says that "at the quantum level, reality is strange and it is nonlocal: the whole universe is a network of time- and space-transcending interconnection."[81] The weird world of the quantum means:

- Each single quantum being in a pure state is considered to be "here" and "there," in other words, everywhere in space and time.
- Each single quantum possesses the state of "potential" up until it becomes "real" due to observation or measurement.
- It is problematic to observe and measure all real states of quanta.
- Quanta, once in a same state, stay linked regardless of distance.

In Laszlo's view, quanta are sociable entities and can remain "entangled" and nonlocally connected irrespective of space and time. He proposes the following: *"Could the nonlocality of the most basic elements of the universe be due to a fundamental field that records the state of particles and atoms and conveys this information to particles and atoms in corresponding states? Could it be that an Akashic Field is active not only at the cosmological scale, but also at the ultra-small scale of physical reality?"*[82] Before suggesting a plausible answer to these questions, he goes on to review the puzzles of biology.

For instance, could the quantum scale characteristics such as coherence and correlation be applied to the functions of living organisms and their environments? In Laszlo's opinion the answer is a definite yes. He argues that if the component parts of any living system do not correlate precisely and flexibly with each other, then the system ultimately breaks down. This explains why current innovative research in quantum biology finds the following:

- That the living organism is fine-tuned and coherent where all constituent elements are multi-dimensionally and instantly correlated
- That the living organism is correlated and coherent with its environment and co-evolves with it

The "adaptive response" of living organisms to environmental input is observed in research tests in which insects or bacteria mutate to counter the effects of toxic exposures. If the interconnectedness of quantum mechanics applies to the living world then the puzzles of biophysics could be explained accordingly. Laszlo ponders, "Could a field, sometimes called 'biofield,' instantly and continuously coordinate the myriad interactions of the organism's myriad molecules, genes, and cells, and correlate entire organisms and species with their environment? Could it be that the Akashic Field we have encountered in microphysics and in cosmology is also active in the domains of life—that it interconnects organisms and ecologies, much as it interconnects quanta at the ultrasmall scale of reality and the universe at the superlarge scale?"[83]

To conclude a concise catalogue of contemporary puzzles, Laszlo looks at current findings in consciousness research:

- Laboratory experiments describe the human capacity for spontaneous transference of thoughts, images, and emotions.

- Native tribes and communities shared information regardless of distance; Information conveyance was denoted in similar customs, architecture, and belief systems.
- The conscious intention and attention of one person may affect another's brain or physical function. The efficacy of such traditional practices is currently confirmed in laboratory experiments providing the foundations for *telesomatic* or nonlocal medicine. Numerous studies and experiments are being carried out to confirm the positive influence of prayer.

In today's scientific literature the connectedness of the human mind is called *transpersonal.* Transpersonal connections are regarded as dubious in modern societies because in general anything that is not manifest to the ordinary somatic senses cannot be accepted as real. Laszlo asks, "Could it be that our consciousness is linked with other consciousnesses through an interconnecting Akashic Field, much as galaxies are linked in the cosmos, quanta in the microworld, and organisms in the world of the living? And could this be the same field we have encountered before, manifesting itself in the realm of mind, in addition to the realms of nature?"[84]

Reviewing the puzzles, it is clear that mainstream scientific theories are not adequate to provide tangible explanations, so these theories are now rendered incomplete. What are the missing factors or aspects that science is not currently considering? Laszlo draws attention to the concepts of connection and correlation. The network of connection accounts for a coherently evolving cosmos, for the entanglement of quanta, for the immediate contact between living organisms and environments, and between the consciousnesses of humans and other animals. Furthermore, besides matter and energy, a subtle element—*information*—serves as an active and dynamic element of the cosmos that connects all things in and through space and time.

The course of the twentieth century saw various terminologies used to describe space-time field such as:

- The luminiferous ether – filled with invisible energy;
- The absolute vacuum – space that is devoid of any matter;
- The cosmic vacuum – far from empty space;
- The unified vacuum – denoting mysterious energy sea;
- The quantum vacuum – physically real cosmic plenum.

Laszlo says, "The quantum vacuum, it appears, transports light, energy, pressure, and sound. Could it have a further property by means of which it correlates separate and possibly distant events? Would it create the correlations that make for the amazing coherence of the quantum, of the organism, of consciousness—and of the whole universe? The vacuum could indeed have such a property. It could be not just a superdense sea of *energy*, but also a sea of *information*."[85]

Laszlo claims that a superdense quantum vacuum generates, conserves, and conveys information. But how can vacuum link and register physical events through space-time? The "torsion-wave" theory, which describes vacuum based vortices, may be the answer to this question. In his view, "*vacuum vortices record information on the state of the particles that created them—and their interference pattern records information on the ensemble of the particles of which the vortices have interfered.* In this way the vacuum records and carries information on atoms, molecules, macromolecules, cells even organisms and populations and ecologies of organisms. There is no evident limit to the information that interfering vacuum torsion waves can conserve and convey. In the final count, they can carry information on the state of the whole universe. Throughout the universe, particles are linked by vacuum in much the same way as objects are linked in the sea: by making and receiving waves."[86]

However, waves have to propagate uninterrupted, otherwise forces cancel them out. In order to justify the eternal wave memory of the universe, vacuum has to be characterized as a frictionless medium. Is that possible? It is possible only if the cosmic vacuum is superdense and superfluid, and also one in which vortices of individual things merge, yet without the information they convey each canceling the other out, so instead they superpose one on the other. Superposed waves are a phenomenon similar to the form of holograms. In a hologram, information is present in every part of it, and Laszlo claims that superposed vacuum-interference waves are nature's holograms. Therefore it must be the quantum vacuum that generates the holographic field serving as the enduring memory of the universe.

Enter the Akashic Field

Laszlo implies that an over-encompassing information field that lies at the very heart of the cosmos is responsible for time- and space-transcending correlations and connections. This superdense, superfluid, and super-rich information field is the holographic memory of the universe. He likens this field to ancient Indian philosophy's concept of the Akashic Record or Akashic Chronicle, which registers everything that happens in the world in the Akashic Field. Laszlo suggests that the Akashic Field (A-field) should be recognized as a valid field alongside the electromagnetic, gravitational, nuclear, and quantum fields. He explains that the A-field is an invisible field. Perceiving the effects of this invisible field is possible, but it cannot be accounted for according to current mainstream scientific theories. A number of puzzles and anomalies in cosmology, quantum physics, biology, and consciousness point to the discovery or rediscovery of an age-old information field that is the Akashic Field.

Laszlo summarizes current research findings in the following fields:

Cosmology

- The Big Bang theory is incomplete.
- The universe is flat.

- The missing mass—one third of the universe— is occupied by visible and invisible matter; the rest appears to be not matter but "dark energy."
- Expansion of the galaxies is accelerating.
- Coherence of cosmic ratios is scale-invariant.
- Cosmic background radiation is uniform in the entire cosmos and the universe evolves as a coherent whole.
- The fine-tuning of cosmic constants allows complex systems to arise and furnishes life.

The universe of universes, the metaverse, is still considered a fable, although it has great explanatory potential. It is more than plausible that our universe is not "all there is"; therefore a metauniverse could possibly be the infinite womb of our universe. Where and how does the A-field fit in? In Laszlo's view, the A-field creates the coherence in our universe and also connects it with prior universes in the metaverse. He argues that at the birth of our universe, vacuum fluctuations were already present that gave rise to our coherent universe, i.e., they must have existed in a pre-vacuum space. The Big Bang did not create vacuum fluctuations; it merely amplified them.

Quantum physics

- superposed wave state—observation and/or measurement "collapse" the superposed wave function of particle into a single determinate state

- indeterminacy and randomness—no physical laws are known to date to predict particle's "collapsed" state
- complementarity and uncertainty principles—particles are either corpuscles or waves, and various states cannot all be measured at the same time

Concepts and theories of quantum physics are advancing at a considerable rate; what were considered a fable yesterday, can be accepted as viable theories tomorrow and vice versa. "Entanglement" and "nonlocality" are not widely recognized in the field of conventional quantum physics, yet Laszlo's Akashic Field theory can account for instant "informational" interaction as the A-field transcends the bounds of space and time, the prerequisite for nonlocal correlation.

BIOLOGY

- Whole system coherence—entire organism is instantly interconnected in a subtle way by multidimensional correlations
- Superconductivity—interlinks biomolecules, cells, and even the whole organism

The interconnected web of life is still being debated. Chance mutation does not account for the great level of complexity achieved in a short period of time. Genetic mutations produce a full set of changes within species because one or a few changes do not bring about positive evolutionary outcome, i.e., a functional mutant. It is suggested that mutations in the genome are highly and quasi-instantly responsive to environmental conditions, meaning that genes and environment are part of an interconnected system. If an organism is considered as a quantum system then it is connected to other organisms and its environment in the same fashion as quanta are connected through space and time, through the information field of the vacuum—the A-field.

Consciousness

- Transpersonal connections—brain/mind of an individual appears to be subtly connected
- Transcultural connections—archeological and historical findings present similar artifacts and buildings across continents disregarding distance and time
- Near-death- and other altered-states-of-consciousness experiences—range of information exchange transcends sensory perception
- Telesomatic connections—effects can be transmitted from one person's mind to another's body

Until now, scientists have not been able to locate the locus and origin of consciousness. Laszlo says that "the recognition that there is a bona fide scientific explanation for the observed nonlocality of consciousness would give legitimacy to research on psi phenomena and open the way to a better understanding of the as yet mysterious dimensions of the human mind. Such explanation is now at hand. The information field that links quanta and galaxies in the physical universe and cells and organisms in the biosphere also links the brains and minds of humans in the sociosphere. This A-field creates the human information pool that Carl Jung* called the collective unconscious and Teilhard de Chardin† called the noosphere and that scientists such as Erwin Schrödinger,‡ David Bohm, William James,§ and Henry Stapp¶ have not hesitated to discuss and to affirm."[87]

How does the A-field work? While the A-field cannot be perceived, its effects can. Just as the gravitational field cannot be perceived but its effect, such as an object falling, can be observed. Laszlo claims that the quantum vacuum produces the A-field, yet how does the A-field's vacuum affect particles and complex things in space and time? The A-field conveys information via superposed vacuum wave-interference patterns that result in correlation and coherence. In Laszlo's view, the A-field's "in-forming" of everything by everything else is *universal* but not *uniform*. Superposed vacuum wave-interference patterns are

---

* Carl Gustav Jung (1875–1961) was a Swiss psychiatrist and psychotherapist who founded analytical psychology. He proposed and elaborated on concepts of extraversion and introversion, archetypes, and the collective consciousness.

† Pierre Teilhard de Chardin (1881–1955) was a French philosopher and Jesuit priest. He was trained as a paleontologist and geologist.

‡ Erwin Rudolf Josef Alexander Schrödinger (1920–1961) was an Austrian physicist. He worked in the field of quantum theory, in particular wave mechanics.

§ William James (1842–1910) was an American philosopher and psychologist who was also trained as a physician.

¶ Henry Stapp (1928–) is an American physicist, works in the field of quantum mechanics.

identical with holograms. In a hologram, every element combines with those that are similar to it, meaning that holographic patterns mesh with similar patterns.

However, this principle does not mean that unlike patterns are not informed. Information is still conveyed, but in a less intense and evident manner than those with corresponding levels. For example, we are directly informed by other humans, but less so by animals, plants and the rest of the world. The A-field's effect is subtle, yet effective; it "fine-tunes" all things, allows life to emerge, and enables stars and galaxies to evolve coherently in the universe.

With regard to the A-field's effects on the living world, Laszlo is convinced that information in and information transmission through the A-field is responsible for not only coherence and correlation within the organism and its environment, but also for the coordination of the creation of life-forms at the primordial stage of the young Earth. He argues that "the mixing of the molecules on the surface of the primeval Earth was not purely random: it was informed by the traces of already evolved life! Evidently, these traces were not those of life on Earth, since we are speaking of the earliest beginnings of biological evolution on this planet. They were the traces of life on other planets."[88]

According to his explanation that torsion-wave interference patterns of particles being carried throughout the universe, the vacuum's hologram life-traces in other regions of the universe could have meshed with life forms emerging on the primeval Earth. "Life on Earth was informed by life elsewhere in the universe—just as Earth life now informs life on other life-bearing planets, wherever they may exist in this galaxy and beyond."[89]

Exploring the Informed Universe

Laszlo explores the cosmologies of the Metaverse or meta-universe. As discussed, the Big Bang theory does not provide a comprehensive theory of the origin and destiny of our universe. Cosmologies of the Metaverse explain that the universe is in fact *the* Metaverse, the mother of our and other universes. Visible, invisible, and subtle energies and information-sea that constitute our universe were present before the Big Bang and will remain after matter created by that explosion vanishes. Laszlo claims that the quantum vacuum is the deeper reality, which pulsates and produces recurring explosions, which then result in local universes. These recurring explosions—Bangs—create particles and antiparticles, which are pulled together by gravitational force into galactic structures. The evolution of universes witnesses galaxies the collapse of galaxies into black holes that in turn lead all galaxies to vanish into supergalactic black holes. These cause "star-bursts," which could account for the Bangs of successive universes.

Metaverse cosmology suggests that each universe leaves its holographic traces in the vacuum, and such traces do not disappear at the birth or death of the universe; traces are superposed and accumulated. In a sense, there is a continuous information transfer between local universes whereby the explosions of "Bangs" amplify the information of the precursor universes. Concerning the birth of our universe, the primeval fluctuations of the vacuum were so highly tuned and precise in order to allow the evolution of life. Accordingly such an occurrence couldn't have been accidental. Conclusively, the vacuum in which our universe emerged was modified by the traces of a previous universe.

If there was a prior universe preceding our universe, then what are the origins of that and of all universes? How did the Metaverse develop? Laszlo replies, "The Metaverse's development also must have been critically influenced by its initial conditions. But prior universes could not have set these conditions, for the Metaverse was there before all universes. How, then, were the initial conditions of the Metaverse determined—*By what* . . . or is the question *By whom*? This is the deepest and greatest mystery of all—the mystery of the origins of the universe-generating process itself."[90]

If we agree that our fine-tuned universe was not an accidental occurrence and a mother universe produces local universes, then "the Metaverse's pre-space was not only such that one universe could arise in it, but also such that an entire series of universes could. This could hardly have been a lucky fluke. We must admit that there must have been an original creative act, an act of 'Metaversal Design.'"[91]

Laszlo clearly does not imply any conservative creationist concept; he merely leaves the question open. The ongoing debate between religious "creationists" and science-influenced "evolutionists" focuses on worldview, whether life evolved or was created. A logical alternative to this debate could be that "design or evolution" is not controversial but that they support one another. This means redefining the dispute from "design *or* evolution" to "design *for* evolution." Suppose the Metaverse came into existence from something and not by pure chance. Suppose the Metaverse was designed, so it could evolve. In this case "design *for* evolution" makes more sense than "design *or* evolution."

Having looked at the origins and the past of the universe, and the Metaverse, what about its future? What is the destiny of the Metaverse and local universes? Destiny follows the path of evolution. "The evolution of the universe has no fixed goal, but it does have a definite direction: toward growing structure and complexity. The evolutionary process adds part to part in coherent and self-consistent wholes. These in turn become part of still other, more encompassing self-consistent wholes."[92] Laszlo says that the evolution of the Metaverse is a cyclic and not a repetitive act. The prior universe informs the successive one, the current universe is always more evolved than the previous one. "Cosmic evolution is toward universes where complex structures emerge, including structures that harbor evolved forms of life—and the evolved forms of mind that are presumably associated with all evolved forms of life."[93]

Laszlo expresses no doubt that suitable conditions are present to furnish life on other planets. According to astronomical analysis, the fundamental constituents of life—hydrogen, oxygen, nitrogen, and carbon—are abundant in the universe, thus allowing complex compounds to occur given the right distribution of such elements with energy. How many life-bearing or life-beholding planets could exist? According to current estimates, there are as many as 100 billion planetary systems in our galaxy and there are just as many galaxies in the universe. If these approximate calculations are correct, then life in the cosmos besides only our planet, is more than possible, it is probable. "In the informed universe, the existence of life, and also of advanced civilizations, is far more probable than in a non-informed universe. Through the A-field, life in any one place informs and facilitates the evolution of life in other places, so the evolution of life never starts from scratch. It is not at the mercy of lucky flukes of random mutations coming up with organisms that prove viable in changing environments."[94]

Having said that universes progress in cyclical fashion and that precise physical resources are required for carbon-based life, it is logical to state that life's span is limited. After a while stars die, black holes decay, and the universe contracts to an evolutionary state, which results in the extinction of life as we know it. But even if a local universe goes through its dying evolutionary phase, the Metaverse remains, and life can evolve again in future universes. Laszlo says that "If evolution in each local universe starts with a clean slate, the evolution of life in local universes is a Sisyphean effort: it breaks down and starts again from scratch, time after time. But local universes are not subject to this ordeal. In each universe, complex systems leave their traces in the vacuum, and the informed vacuum of one universe informs the evolution of the next.

"Consequently, each universe creates conditions favorable to the evolution of life in successive universes. In each successive universe, life evolves more and more efficiently, and thus in equal times evolves further and further. This is a cyclical process with a learning curve. Each universe starts without life, evolves life when some planets become capable of supporting it, and wipes it out when planetary conditions pass beyond the life-supporting stage. But the vacuum shared by all the universes records and conserves the wave-form traces of the life that evolved in each universe! The vacuum becomes more and more informed *with* life, and therefore more and more informing *of* life."[95]

Laszlo's thought process corresponds with Indian philosophy's Akasha. There, the cycles of life—the *samsara** that denotes "being-to-becoming" and again of "becoming-to-being"—are subsumed. All the myriad aspects of the manifest world fuse into a state that is over and above distinguishable aspects into the state of Brahman, the absolute reality. All aspects of the manifest world are secondary aspects and reflections of an underlying quantum vacuum, a subtle energy and information plenum—the *Metaverse,* to use Laszlo's terminology. The manifest world is considered an illusion, *maya,*† in Indian philosophy. The absolute reality of Brahman supervenes, and the manifest world constantly co-creates the non-duality of the universe—the *advaita.*‡

* Samsara is a Sanskrit word means the repeating cycle of birth, life, and death.

† Maya is a Sanskrit word meaning illusion or delusion.

‡ Advaita is a Sanskrit word that means "not two," non duality.

Following Laszlo's views on the existence of the Metaverse, space can no longer be viewed according to the Newtonian concept. Space is not an empty or passive domain, on the contrary. The primary reality of the universe is the unified vacuum, from which universes originate and into which they die. Matter is the hologram-like aggregated product of quantum probability arising out of the infinite and fundamental information-energy plenum.

Considering all that has been discussed above, where does human and cosmic consciousness fit into the informed universe? The Integral Theory of Everything needs to account for the phenomena of consciousness, for otherwise the theory is incomplete; it is not integral. Contrary to general belief, consciousness does not reside in the brain. Medical science has not detected any area of the brain that is responsible for generating consciousness. Brain function and states of consciousness are correlated, but the former does not produce the latter. Laszlo says that "in the final count we must recognize that all the things that arise and evolve in the universe have both a matter-aspect and a mind-aspect. All things in the world—quanta and galaxies, molecules, cells, and organisms—have 'materiality' as well as 'interiority.' Matter and mind are not separate, distinct realities; they are aspects of a deeper reality that has both an external matter-aspect, and an internal mind-aspect."[96]

Everyday human experience is dominated by information conveyed by the five senses: the sounds, smells, flavors, sights, and textures of the world that surrounds us. Sensory information is processed by neurons connected by synapses, the neuroaxonal network, in the brain. Conventional science maintains that this is the only information we receive from the world beyond the body. Innovative neuroscience explains that humans are capable of perceiving information in addition to the five senses, as there is a vast hierarchy of other networks besides the brain's neuroaxonal network extending all the way to quantum dimensions. Cutting-edge tests confirm that humans are able to pick up quantum-resonance based information that originates beyond the manifest world. But besides picking up quantum signals, is it correct to suggest that humans can send such signals too?

As Laszlo explained, quantum waves propagate in the cosmos, so it is logical to say that these waves interfere with the waves generated by the human body and mind, which in turn bring about complex holograms. "Generations after generations of humans have left their holographic traces in the A-field. These individual holograms integrate in a superhologram, which is the encompassing hologram of a tribe, community, or culture. The collective holograms interface and integrate in turn with the super-superhologram of all people. This is the collective information pool of humankind."[97]

If there is such an information locus, how can one extract all things or events embedded in it? Laszlo is convinced that "we can read the information carried by these holograms. On the principle of 'like informs like,' we can read first of all the information carried by the hologram of our own brain and body. Reading *out* what we have read *into* the field is the physical basis of long-term memory. It removes the limitation on information storage by a brain enclosed in a finite cranium. We can read out anything and everything that we have read into the field—we can literally 're-call' from it all the things we have ever experienced."[98]

In conclusion, reading-into this information field may be the explanation of mystical or prophetic insights that appear not in words per se but in intuitions, visions, and sensations. The human brain restricts and selects the overwhelming volume of information entering our conscious awareness in order to preserve our mental stability. When accessing altered-states of consciousness—such as deep prayer, meditation, and hypnogogic and hypnopompic states—quantum-based information is not repressed in such states or blocked by the brain's filters and thus can reach our conscious awareness.

Human consciousness is not static, not fixed once and for all. It is a product of long evolutionary development, and is capable of further progress. It is interesting to note that the human body did not change greatly in comparison to human consciousness in the course of the fifty thousand-year history of the species. According to indigenous cultures such as the Native Americans, periodically new consciousness arises that brings fundamental transformation of the world. The definition and characterization of the particular stages of the evolution of consciousness was explained by the Indian thinker Sri Aurobindo.* He suggested that humans undertake psychic, spiritual, and supramental transformations towards self-discovery

* Sri Aurobindo (1872–1950) was an Indian philosopher, poet, and freedom fighter.

in order to uncover the divine nature of life and cosmic superconsciousness. Ken Wilber* worked extensively on mapping the evolutionary steps and aspects of human consciousness. Chris Cowan† and Don Beck‡ argue that human nature is not fixed, and humans are able to adapt to environmental and life conditions to construct new conceptual models to solve problems. Cowan and Beck formulated a colorful "spiral dynamics" depicting layers of humans values and different stages of the evolving consciousness.

Explanations of the meaning, direction, and path of human conscious evolution share a common attribute: progress from ego-based to transpersonal-based consciousness. Laszlo is an advocate of transpersonal-consciousness as it would furnish a positive effect towards creating a sustainable planet and understanding our world in its entirety. "A society hallmarked by transpersonal consciousness is not likely to be materialistic and self-centered; it would be more deeply and widely informed. Under the impact of a more evolved consciousness, the system of nation-states would transform into a more inclusive and coordinated system with due respect for diversity and the right of all peoples and cultures to self-determination. Economic systems would remain diversified but not fragmented; they would combine local autonomy with global coordination and pursue goals

* Kenneth Earl Wilber II (1949–) is an American writer focusing on mysticism, ecology, philosophy, and developmental psychology.

† Christopher C. Cowan (birthdate undisclosed) is an American theorist.

‡ Don Edward Beck (1937–) is an American theorist, focusing on evolutionary and organizational psychology.

that serve all the peoples and countries of the world, whatever their creed, level of economic development, population size, and natural resource endowment. As a result, disparities in wealth and power would be moderated and frustration and resentment would diminish, together with crime, terrorism, war, and other forms of violence. Societies would become peaceful and sustainable, offering a fair chance of life and well-being to all their members, living and yet to be born."[99]

Following the proposition of cutting-edge neuroscientists and philosophers that consciousness is not located or produced by the brain, could human consciousness survive physical death? Is human consciousness immortal? People claim to perceive things in states of near-death, past-life, and out-of-body experiences, as well as mystical and religious experiences. In each of these cases, people speak of vivid events that are not experienced in normal states of conscious awareness. Having ascertained before that it is possible to reading the information field's holographic traces left by previous events, it is logical to suggest that retrieving elements of such events is also plausible. The A-field retains the complex holograms of every event and experience, every human and every community. Information stored in the A-field is encoded infinitely. Laszlo concludes that "we as individuals are not immortal, but our experience is. The traces of everything we have ever experienced persist, and they can be forever recalled."[100]

Reading-in the A-field is exemplified by practices such as past-life regression therapy. Through hypnosis or certain breathing exercises, the client or patient speak of re-experiencing "past-life events." Researchers like Ian Stevenson* have investigated thousands of cases of children who claimed to remember past lives. Children recounted clear memories of others and events which held no relevance to their current life experiences. Stevenson believed that mental or physical injuries, birthmarks, or ailments were not necessarily due to hereditary factors but rather past lives. If these interpretations are correct, then the notion that one can read-in the information field by quantum signals entering our consciousness is more than possible.

Laszlo says that "the information carried in the vacuum's A-field is active and effective. Its range is vast; it embraces other humans as well as other forms of life, and all things in the universe. In integrating with it, it is not our individual body and our individual soul, but our individual *experience* that achieves immortality. We do not disappear from the world without a trace; all that we experience becomes part of the collective memory bank of humankind, to be read out again and again. We can live on in the brain and consciousness of people today, and in all future generations."[101]

Concluding remarks on *Science* and the *Akashic* Field

In summary, the Akashic Field suggests the existence of an informed universe where information rather than matter is the fundamental feature. Everything that happens in the A-field affects—"informs"—everything else. Laszlo explains that our

* Ian Stevenson (1918–2007) was a Canadian-American psychiatrist known for reincarnation research.

world is not just things moving about in space and time, that is, only the surface. Below there is an interconnected, holographically "in-formed," and fundamentally whole world where all things interpenetrate with all other things. Our universe can be understood as an all-pervasive consciousness that expresses itself in space and time, energy, and matter through geometric patterns on all scales of existence.

Laszlo recognizes that there is a new science emerging with principles and assumptions compatible with systems thinking. Conventional science regards nature as objects and seeks power over it, whereas this new science regards nature as connections and seeks partnership with it. Conventional science is reductionist whereas the new science is integral. Laszlo's new science looks at the world in a different way from conventional science. The main feature of the new view is that there is a "real" dimension of the universe, which is not observable. This unobservable dimension is the ultimate reality; it serves as the foundation of the observable universe whereas the observed phenomena are its manifestation.

This "hidden" dimension is not new to science and philosophy; it was rediscovered in the twentieth century by theoretical physicists to identify the fields and forces of nature with universal origins in a unified, grand-unified and super-grand-unified field. David Bohm spoke of the "implicate order," an unobservable holofield, the womb of quantum phenomena from which the "explicate order" arises. The "hidden" dimension creates enduring nonlocal connections in space and time. Spacetime is an interconnecting memory-medium with infinite memory capacity. Traditional cosmologies, such as Hindu, recognized the existence of the interconnecting memory-medium as a fundamental dimension called Akasha. Cutting-edge theoreticians explain an underlying domain beyond the observed entities and forces called the zero-point field, quantum vacuum, cosmic plenum or grand-unified field. This underlying field is recognized as the primeval field that had created the spacetime of our universe.

Spatial and temporal entanglement on the macroscopic and microscopic levels suggests precise coordination, connection and space- and time-transcending information exchange between complex systems of universes, galaxies, planets, and humans alike. Precise coherence and consistency assures the evolution of: universes, galaxies, planets, and humans alike.

Laszlo's theories, developed in dozens of books and publication over four decades, are "connecting the dots" in regard to the findings that are coming to light at the cutting edge of science and consolidating them into a relevant new paradigm. Laszlo recognized that the "Akashic field" needs to be further researched, developed, articulated, and presented to science as a contribution toward reaching an integral understanding in the natural and humanistic disciplines, and in society as a conceptual orientation that endeavors to achieve higher levels of sustainability and well-being. He recognized that a full understanding of the A-field has major implications for humans. It changes the way humans view themselves and the world, and in the final count changes their aspirations and their expectations for themselves and the world. The A-field denotes the next evolution of thinking and consciousness.

Two Aspects of One Coherent Whole

The bridging of science and spirituality is further explored and elaborated in the next book Laszlo published in 2006 titled *Science and the Reenchantement of the Cosmos: The Rise of the Integral Vision of Reality*. Laszlo argues that science is on the brink of a paradigm shift, which is being brought about by the rediscovery of a fundamental cosmic field, the Akashic field (A-field). The gap between science and spirituality is being bridged by a revolutionary new theory—the Theory of Everything—which uncovers the effects of nonlocalized consciousness and the way in which the material world and spiritual experience are two aspects of one coherent whole. All the basic scientific premises with regard to the nature of matter and reality are under revision because established theories cannot account for all the phenomena in the universe, but Laszlo states that the concept of the Akashic field can accomplish this.

In his view, this field sheds a full light on our cosmos, a cosmos that is a dynamic and a quasi-self-evolving system; where everything is interconnected and integral with everything else at all scales and domains. This fundamental field conveys and conserves energy and information with consciousness being as fundamental as energy and more fundamental than matter. Uncovering and understanding the coherent unity of the cosmos and humankind within it allows a dialogue between science and spirituality for a possible reunion between them. The ancient concept of the unity of consciousness or Oneness expressed in Hinduism, Daoism, and Buddhism has found a modern expression in Laszlo's Metaverse, the mother of all universes known as the Akashic field. Laszlo posits that the universe is *reenchanted*, informationally encapsulated, and interconnected in a mysterious way.

The amazing coherence of body, mind, and cosmos is discussed in the first part of *Science and the Reenchantement of the Cosmos: The Rise of the Integral Vision of Reality.* The emerging, integral nature of reality describes our universe as meaningful and not disenchanted. It is reenchanted in a sense that our world "is a harmonious structure where all things interact with all other things and together create a coherent whole. This whole is not a mechanical aggregate, for it is not readily decomposable to its parts. It is an integral whole, where to some extent and in some way all things interact with all other things. The scope of this interaction transcends the hitherto known limits of time and space. It is nearly instantaneous over any known distance and is conserved over any known span of time."[102]

The amazing coherence of the body or any living organism is structured at a high level of coherence. If it were not so, the body or living organism could not function optimally; it would break down and result in ill health or death. This high degree of coherence extends to every level of the living organism, from micro-molecules and cells to organs and other parts, encompassing the entirety of the organism. All elements are in constant communication with each other for maintenance, and for applying changes as necessary to retain the coherent state of the organism.

Coherence in the cosmic scale is as harmonious as in living systems. Universal constants are finely tuned to allow the emergence and evolution of life. Laszlo says that ". . . this is still not all. It turns out that galaxies evolve nearly uniformly in all directions from Earth, a finding that is surprising, because not all parts of the universe are connected by light, the fastest form of physical signal-transmission according to Einstein's theory of relativity. At its periphery the universe expands beyond the 13.7 billion light years that rays of light could have traveled in the time that has elapsed since the Big Bang—and yet galactic evolution is consistent throughout the universe."[103]

Coherence between the human body and its environment is also finely tuned. Genome* and phenome† are not fully separate as previously thought by Darwin. Contrary to the Darwinian concept, Laszlo argues that genome is receptive to external impact and for this reason higher multi-cellular species evolved from simple origins in a short time-frame, which could not have happened if the genome had been isolated since its random mutation would have taken a much longer time to produce viable species on Earth.

Coherence between human mind and the universe is as harmonious as between living organisms and the world. Humans

---

* Genome – set of molecules in the DNA that conveys information to the cells needs to build the entire organism.

† Phenome – represents the sum total of an organism's phenotypic traits. Although any phenotype of any organism has a basis in its genotype, phenotypic expression may be influenced by environmental influences, mutation, and genetic variation. (http://en.wikipedia.org/wiki/Phenome)

are capable of receiving information originating from the external world not only through our five senses but also directly through, or into, the mind. Extra or non-sensory perception and practices are documented in various cultures throughout human history. Shamans, as medicine men, heal via the transmission of information that exceeds material forms.

Laszlo affirms that "of course, not every single thing we could name is coherent with every other single thing—that is more than the evidence speaks to. Pebbles, rocks, and mountains are not necessarily and intrinsically coherent with each other and with other things around them. But the particles that make up the atoms that make up the pebbles, the rocks, and the mountains are in fact coherent with each other—and so are the trees that grow on the side of the mountains and the organisms including us humans who walk on the pebbles and mountains. Universal coherence is a fundamental finding, and it gives us a fundamentally new concept of the nature of reality."[104]

These arguments raise the question: What element is responsible for connections and coherence in an evolving cosmos? Is there a common ground on which instant connections between organisms, environment and consciousness rest upon? Laszlo suggests there must be a fundamental field, an all-encompassing medium that underlies all things, a medium that in fact also *becomes* all things. This insight has been acknowledged and presented by ancient traditions, especially Hinduism, which calls this fundamental field, the Akasha, one among five elements in the cosmos. The other four are: air, fire, water, and earth. Philosophers and scientists alike throughout history have known about the fifth element. Aristotle called it the "aether"; Nikola Tesla the "original medium" and modern science names it the "quantum vacuum" or "unified vacuum." Laszlo named this field the Akashic field, which conserves and conveys information just as it connects and correlates. "The current rediscovery of the Akashic Field as a cosmic holofield reinforces qualitative human experience with quantitative data generated by sciences experimental method. The combination of unique personal insight and interpersonally observable and repeatable experience gives us the best assurance we can have that we are on the right track: an A-field connects organisms and minds in the biosphere and particles, stars, and galaxies throughout the universe. This transforms a machine-like universe that is blindly groping its way from one phase of its evolution to the next into a whole-system universe that builds on the information it has itself generated. The world is more like a living organism than a machine. It evolves from the present toward the future on the basis of its evolution from the past to the present. Its logic is the logic of life itself: evolution toward coherence and wholeness, through interconnection and interaction."[105]

Laszlo asserts that our universe is not a *matter of chance*; it is a *matter of inheritance*. The Metaverse, a cyclically universe-creating plenum informs forthcoming universes by the trace information of prior universes. In his view, Metaverse evolves toward life and consciousness in universe after universe. Consciousness infuses all things in the cosmos and is as fundamental as energy. Laszlo agrees with Plato and Whitehead concerning the doctrine of *panpsychism*. "The panpsychism thesis of universal consciousness is not the thesis that consciousness of the kind I myself experience is universal. Rather, it is the thesis that the roots and potentials of the kind of consciousness I experience are inherent in every particle and every atom in the cosmos. It is the thesis that consciousness evolves: it takes on complex forms in complex systems."[106] According to this thesis, the cosmos has a psychophysical character with an equal division into physical and mental aspects.

Laszlo poses an existential question in terms of his integral worldview. Coherence or the lack of it determines the functioning of the system. In an interconnected universe where humans have the ability to access certain aspects of each other's consciousness, human conscious choice is decisive toward coherent well-being, and a coherently functioning society and environment. "Our ability to consciously intend action that promotes coherence in and around us endows our life with a moral dimension. We not only behold the world; we participate in it—and we can choose to participate in it well. Choosing to do so makes us healthy and whole, creative elements in an integrally evolving universe."[107]

Laszlo's scientific-spiritual worldview explains that humans have the privilege and responsibility to make conscious choices in their lives. To determine what is a right or wrong choice depends on *coherence*. As stated previously, a wrong choice may result in ill health, on account of which the body can't function coherently. A right choice in community and environment results in the optimal functioning of a coherent society and planet.

While mainstream science disregards the spiritual non-manifest dimension of reality, Laszlo argues that physical reality extends beyond human sensory experience, that is, to a form that is consciousness, thus concluding that reality is *psychophysical.* He posits that "human consciousness is a high-level articulation of the consciousness that stems from, and is rooted in, the quantum vacuum; the superfluid universal field that is the fundamental element of the integral element of the integral reality of the psychophysical cosmos."[108]

This information based, holographically interconnected Akashic field provides a solid foundation for a unifying and integrative "Theory of Everything."

CHAPTER 10

Laszlo's Evolutionary Systems Views on the Challenge of the Third Millennium

In the late nineteen-seventies, besides his continuing academic research, Laszlo held appointments at various universities in the USA. He held positions as Professor of Philosophy at the State University of New York, visiting Professor of Music and Aesthetics at Indiana University, visiting Professor of Philosophy at Northwestern University, visiting Professor of Future Studies at the University of Houston, and visiting Professor of Systems Studies at the University of Portland. He served as a Fellow of Yale University and the Princeton Center of International Studies.

His public assignments included Founder and Director of the General Evolution Research Group,* then Special Fellow at the United Nations Institute for Training and Research

* *General Evolutionary Research Group* was founded in 1984 by Ervin Laszlo; cofounders were Riane Eisler, Cultural Historian; David Loye, psychologist and system scientist; Ralph Abraham, Mathematician and Chaos theorist; Eric Chaisson, astrophysicist; Gyorgy Kampis, computer scientist; and Vilmos Csanyi, biologist.

(UNITAR), which was followed by becoming program director of the Institute's project on the New International Economic Order. His seven-year tenure at the United Nations produced fifteen volumes on the New International Economic Order and another six volumes on Regional and International Cooperation. In the mid-eighties Laszlo travelled extensively, giving seminars and lectures as well as responding to calls for advice and collaboration with Federico Mayor, the Director-General of UNESCO.

In 1993 Laszlo was one of the keynote speakers at the Third World Congress of the World Federation of Hungarians. Then he suggested that Hungary become the host to an international artists and writers club to aid the works of the Club of Rome on the world's economic and political problems with a focus on the urgent need of new thinking, and revaluation of personal and global responsibilities. The Hungarian government welcomed his idea, and in the same year set up a secretariat of the worldwide organization called the Club of Budapest for which Laszlo served and still serves as Founder/President. Laszlo's first report to the Club titled *The 3rd Millennium: The Challenge and the Vision* that was published in 1997.

The works of the Club of Rome presented humanity with a warning regarding the limits to growth. *Goals for Mankind*, his first report for the Club of Rome, called for the recognition of the importance of human consciousness and for the need for consciousness to evolve, the need to live more wisely, more responsively individually and globally in the coming third millennium. Almost twenty years separate the two clubs' reports, and the world has indeed changed at an ever-accelerating rate and on a larger scale than ever before. The global population has greatly increased; ineffective social, political and technological practices have put more demands and pressures on every sphere of life—while adversely impacting the environment. New conditions necessitate new ways of thinking, a new understanding of and vision for humanity, nature and the world as a whole. This new vision, Laszlo said, calls for new ethics, new values and new modes of life. The first report of the Club of Budapest presents these concepts, which also constitute the subject of this chapter.

Where are we now and where will we be if we do or if we don't change the directions of our lives? Close to the turn of another century, the world is fraught with problems. Economic growth's shadow points to increasing global unemployment; nuclear power not only supplies energy, but its waste affects the environment adversely; modern medicine is unable to tackle the HIV/AIDS epidemic; information technology connects people around the planet and gives access to worldwide information with the downside of giving rise to a new medium for crime—for example Internet-based pornography and drugs/arms trafficking that influence people's lives globally. Humanity is approaching a critical turning point due to this progression, which is not sustainable, let alone tolerable.

In *The 3rd Millennium* Laszlo says, "The size of the human population, multiplied by the amount of resources it uses and the waste and pollution it generates, specifies the load placed on the planet's physical resources and biological systems. But the physical resources are in finite supply, and the biological life-support systems are progressively impaired. Given the continuation of these trends, it is merely a matter of time before the two curves will intersect. At that point humanity's demands will exceed the planet's existing supplies and potentially regenerative capacities. We are already feeling the approach of this critical threshold—not only in the environmental domain, but also in the spheres of production, consumption, politics, personal lifestyles, employment, professional goals, and community life."[109] This impact on the planet and human lives cannot increase indefinitely, states Laszlo. The Club of Rome's publication *The Limits to Growth* did not achieve its desired outcome because people viewed it as a mere theoretical concept, irrelevant to human lives. In general, humankind did not accept the report's conclusion that there are absolute limits to socio-economic development. And even where they did, most people considered the report's conclusions to be so futuristic that they were irrelevant to today's reality, and their attitude was "why should we change"?

It is undeniable that there is a general widening gap between rich and poor, that income distribution is unequal and accelerating population growth and urbanization deplete environmental resources. The solution must be to live more responsibly, to modify production and consumption by taking into account the ecosystem's limits. Laszlo suggests the following orientations:

- Reduce emissions of CO_2 and other greenhouse gases into the atmosphere
- Reforest denuded lands and prevent erosion of cultivable lands
- Reduce and clean up pollution
- Develop alternative fuels
- Do away with weapons of mass destruction and dangerous technologies
- Reduce the gap between the rich and the poor
- Inhibit conspicuous consumption
- Provide better living and working conditions for women
- Encourage a reverse flow of people from the cities back to the countryside
- Retrain the unemployed and the underemployed
- Facilitate environment-friendly business ventures
- Reallocate resources in favor of education and health care
- Encourage smaller families[110]

The issue is not just whether humanity *could* but also more to the point is whether it *should* change in these directions. Responsibility for doing so lies in the hands of individuals: they need to think globally. The benefit of that, says Laszlo, is to reorient one's perspective towards making wise choices in regard to processes rather than structures, dynamic wholes rather than stagnant parts. In other words, a person thinking globally sees the whole reality rather than just segments of it. "Global thinking is not a personal matter, and not a mere utopia. It can be practiced, and when practiced, it can have major and otherwise unattainable effects. This embraces impacts on land-use, on agricultural production and trade, on transportation systems, and on all things that affect the life and wellbeing of people in today's technological societies."[111]

Responsible decisions require constant questioning of ourselves and the making of considered individual choices followed by corresponding action. Is the profession I choose just a means of individual financial gain or is it useful for myself and others? Will the choice of this consumer product contribute to pollution of the environment and create more waste? Do I make choices that enhance simultaneously my own and others' lives? Does my life and lifestyle allow others to live the way they want?

Individual responsibility for global thinking and behavior is one aspect of the needed change. Enterprises and business ventures must follow the same principles as responsible individuals. Profit and growth need to contribute to the greater good of all. Focusing only on shareholder benefit must be replaced with a different value that benefits of all people within the organization. "Hierarchical structures are increasingly inefficient—they have to be replaced by lean organizational modalities and reliance on partner- and staff-consultation based on two-way flows of information and communication."[112] Laszlo does not stop at this level, he further addresses a plethora of political, leadership and governmental issues. Political leaders need to adhere to the same responsible and ethical rules and behaviors as individuals and private enterprises.

National governments need to consider decentralizing their powers with regard to conditions that affect employment, social security, and justice as well as ethnic groups and minorities. Creating regional defense pacts with other countries can scale down the size and the expenditure of national armies. It is not a utopia to create good external relations with neighboring countries and good internal security in each country through a well-equipped National Guard or police force.

The health of the environment has to be considered of equal importance with national security and the well-being of citizens. Safeguarding and preserving national resources is vital for a healthy and sustainable environment and for society at large.

Laszlo points out clearly that humanity has two choices: Either it creates a sustainable global civilization or it heads toward massive global ecological crises and catastrophes. He is pragmatic—our future is at stake. Moral codes that spell out the norms of responsible behavior need to be adopted. Such codes can guide people's goals and aspirations. The world's great religions set out moral codes, such as the Ten Commandments of Jews and Christians, the codes of Islam taught in the Koran, and the teachings of the moral principles of the Buddhism. But science has not provided society with an authoritative ethical code. Attempts were made toward the development of positive ethical codes by Saint-Simon,* Auguste Comte,† and Emile Durkheim,‡ but such trends did not become mainstream in twentieth-century science. A sound ethical code would create sound environmental practices that in turn could promote healthy processes in nature and society. Individual and social behavior must adopt an ethical code, which will establish "an enduring equilibrium between the requirements of individual, social, and economic development, and the regenerative capacities of the biosphere's systems of water, air, energy, and land."[113]

How is it possible to find unity in the diversity of cultures in the world? According to Laszlo the basic requirement is for each culture to evolve within its own legal/moral/historical/religious tradition while allowing its people to live in harmony with other cultures. The clash of cultures affects peace in the world even more than the inflexibility of nation-states. Unity allied to cultural diversity entails mutual tolerance and mutually beneficial cooperation, which creates a culture of interexistence with active, participatory and harmonious relationships.

* Claude Henri de Rouvroy, Comte de Saint-Simon (1760–1825) was a French philosopher and economist.

† Isidore Auguste Marie François Comte (1798–1857) was a French philosopher who worked on the doctrine of positivism and the discipline of sociology.

‡ David Émile Durkheim (1858–1917) was a French sociologist, social psychologist, and philosopher. He is considered of one of the founder of modern social science and sociology.

Creative Paths of Human Evolution— A New Vision for Our Time

A *new vision* is called for to overcome the great challenges faced by humanity. This new vision points to an interconnected whole-system within which there is unity in diversity in every sphere of life.

The vision of science needs to be revised. The current vision of science impels humankind toward a dehumanizing world that functions as a soulless machine where life is a random accident. In Laszlo's view, there is no categorical divide between the physical and the living world, on one hand, and the world of mind and consciousness on the other. Interdisciplinary research programs can connect the life sciences with the physical and the cognitive sciences; and the theories of evolutionary systems with chaos theories. Systemic concepts apply equally to physical, biological, psychological, and sociological phenomena.

Laszlo criticizes philosophers, sociologists, and scientists for waging unnecessary "paradigm- and science-wars." Such wars do not further the advancement of a new scientific vision to gain deeper insight into the nature of the world and the role of humans within the world. "Helping people to catch up with the world picture of front-line science is a moral responsibility for everybody who is concerned with, or about, the role of science in society. Scientists and the philosophers of science need to realize that science is not only a source of technology, and not only of concern to their specialized communities: it is also a source of meaning and a guide to life, and as such of concern to everyone. Science administrators, science journalists, and the media as a whole, share the responsibility for effectively communication the emerging insights. The responsibility is also shared by educators at all levels, from the kindergarten through graduate school and adult education."[114]

Artists have the same responsibility as scientists, philosophers, and sociologists. Art as a human activity can portray and promote the *new vision* by penetrating the deep regions of the human psyche. The responsibility of religious leaders is to communicate the spirit and meaning of their scriptures, not their words, as their literal interpretation can lead to misinterpretation, conflict, and dogmatism. According to Laszlo the original intention behind religious rites and rituals was to serve as inspiration for the followers to conduct a moral life with love and care for all. Competition between faiths turned attention away from the concept of oneness and humility, the underpinnings of genuine religious and spiritual experience.

In *The 3rd Millennium: The Challenge and the Vision,* Laszlo summarizes the basics requirements of action in the next century. First and foremost, humanity needs to guide its own evolution consciously. Systemic processes underlie all forms of evolution in nature. The underlying dynamics are nonlinear and have a particular logic of their own. Humanity's task is to facilitate the unfolding of basic evolutionary processes in society. This is not a passive process; it means on the contrary that humans play their own part in fostering the processes of conscious evolution. Ethical living is a necessity, but it is not the whole requirement. Egoistic behavior must be replaced by broader human-, nature-, and planet-centered behaviors. The only way humankind can achieve global-scale economic, social, and ecological transformation is by transforming itself. Laszlo claims, "The way to conscious evolution is through an evolved consciousness."[115] Humans have changed their surroundings, but now they are gradually also changing themselves: an evolved consciousness is arising.

"The stakes are high. Without a new consciousness it is unlikely that we will be able to avert deepening economic, social, and cultural conflicts and ecological breakdowns. But if our consciousness is able to move up from the self-centered and parochial to the planet-centered and universally human dimension, our economic power and technological sophistication will be matched with a deeper spiritual and emotional maturity. This is the creative evolution we need in order to consciously evolve our world, and bring ourselves and our children safely to a soft landing in the post-modern age of the third millennium."[116]

Once people understand the new insights emerging in science they will look at themselves and the world around them differently. The latest theories in science speak of the observable universe as a manifestation of a holistic, holographic quasi-infinite virtual-energy sea in what is misleadingly termed the "vacuum." The holographic nature of the energy sea provides interconnection between all things and processes in the manifest world, whether they are physical, biological, social, or cultural. The emerging vision in physics tells us the following:

- matter is a product of the vacuum's zero-point field
- there is no absolute matter, only an absolute matter-generating virtual-energy field
- physical reality is not material
- mass-particles are standing waves in the space-time-filling quantum vacuum
- chance alone does not account for the emergence of life
- specific fields are responsible for information linkages
- humans are affected by subtle energies in the biosphere
- human interaction and communication extend beyond the five senses

The Philosophy, the Aims, and the Objectives of the Club of Budapest

Laszlo founded the Club of Budapest organization in 1993 with a main objective to catalyze recognition of the urgent need to evolve a new consciousness through various projects. These projects include initiatives communicating and promoting new scientific insights, helping business organizations to pursue ethical and globally-effective initiatives while also assisting projects that further new thinking in the spheres of art, education, and spirituality. The Club is committed to identifying those individuals and organizations who carry out and promote evolved consciousness practices, and to recognize them by awarding an annual "Planetary Consciousness Prize." Laszlo invited honorary members to support the club's cause who were internationally renowned artists, visionaries, politicians, scientists, and philosophers. These members were, and many still are, engaged with the club and its mission.

The new insights into the nature of matter, life, and the mind presented by Laszlo give humanity a new sense of the significance of the role it plays in its own evolution. Humans are equipped with the ability to know and plan their actions rather than being passive agents. Laszlo emphasizes the positive aspects of individuality, innovation, and diversity as the basis for harmony, cooperation, and coevolution. He points out that humanity needs a new global awareness for the new millennium, grounded in new ways of thinking and assuming local and global ethical responsibility for one's action while harnessing the richness of humanity's cultural diversity. Laszlo's action plan is for a new planetary consciousness with less self-centered behavior and more collective- and nature-centered living, so as to create a cooperative and consciously evolving global society.

Macroshift

Macroshift: Navigating the Transformation to a Sustainable World was published in 2001. This book is an enlarged and updated version of the first report of the Club of Budapest, *The 3rd Millennium: The Challenge and The Vision. Macroshift* is an excellent synthesis describing a globalized world and providing a profound exploration of the current transition describing a globalized world. Laszlo calls on humans to be creative and innovative participants in making the shift towards a new culture and consciousness to create a sustainable and meaningful future for humankind.

The signs and manifestations of the need for transformation are global, such as epidemic disease, environmental degradation, nuclear plant pollution, over-mechanized agriculture, famine, inequality in material standards of living, and over-population of the planet, to name but a few. History has produced other macroshifts, but they occurred over centuries whereas the current Macroshift, driven by the speed and power of technology is compressed into a few generations at most. The macroshift now envisaged presents humans with an opportunity to collectively overcome dangerous global problems, since it will impact their thinking and behavior in such a way as to lead to a more humane and sustainable global future. In this book, Laszlo demonstrates a real insight and a clear understanding of the complexity of natural evolution and the complexity of current social and cultural issues. He employs his profound understanding of systems theory incorporating comments by some of the Honorary Members of the Club of Budapest, to offer a practical guide for directing the course of the outcome of a new Macroshift.

The World in Macroshift and the Ways Ahead

Laszlo begins by reviewing the nature and dynamics of macroshifts, and then he describes what are the necessary factors and preconditions for these shifts to take place in history and how the current shift is developing in the contemporary world. He calls on the language of systems theory to give deeper insights into the developmental dynamics of any system in regard to future predictions of societal transitions and possible outcomes. "Given the unsustainability of many trends and processes in today's world, the dynamic of development that will apply to our future is not the linear dynamic of classical extrapolation but the nonlinear chaos dynamic of complex-system evolution."[117] According to systems and chaos theory, nonlinear development means that "the evolution of complex systems always involves alternating periods of stability and instability, continuity and discontinuity, order and chaos. We are at the threshold of a period of instability today—a period of chaos."[118]

In Laszlo's view, the current Macroshift is in fact a bifurcation, using Prigogine's terminology. Various attractors affect the outcome of any bifurcation. According to Laszlo, one attractor is human consciousness. "In periods of relative stability the consciousness of individuals does not play a decisive role in society's evolution, but in periods of chaos it does. When a human society reaches the limits of its stability, it becomes supersensitive and is highly responsive to the smallest fluctuation. Then the system responds to even subtle changes in values, beliefs, worldviews, and aspirations. A Macroshift is a process of societal evolution in which the limits of the system's stability initiates a bifurcation: an era of transformation. This is an era of unprecedented freedom to decide the system's future."[119]

"The Macroshift moves toward a successful conclusion if, and only if, a critical mass of people in society evolve their mindset. They must generate and embrace values, worldviews, and ethics that mesh with the conditions that were inadvertently spawned by the technological innovations of their predecessors. How soon and indeed whether a critical mass evolves its values, worldviews, and consciousness is not written in the stars. It depends on the variety of the people and the flexibility of the dominant institutions. These vary from age to age, culture to culture, and society to society."[120] Laszlo concludes that technological innovations destabilize existing structures, which leads to macroshifts. Thus technology can be considered as the motor for macroshifts, and the shift in the values and consciousness of a critical mass of people determines in which direction the transformation goes.

Laszlo then discusses various macroshifts in history. Neolithic people understood, and lived by, a sacred dimension of the world. Their cultures and communities viewed space and time as part of the natural order where spirit was not separated from matter. Seen and unseen forces were integral parts of their lives, which generated profound empathy with all they encountered.

Archaic empires like Mesopotamia, Babylonia, Egypt, and China followed. The Stone Age of *Mythos* was followed by the archaic world of *Theos*. The way of life changed to a more hierarchical order and a division of labor. The cosmos was considered as a sovereign power ruling and regulating the whole universe and everything in it. Then values and ethical codes as well as the worldview changed again. Greek and Roman civilizations were affected by technological advances, which reflected in their social structures. Theory-based observation, elaborated by reasoning, replaced mythical concepts. *Logos* took hold in the Hellenic era, and was later modified by Christianity. In the West, medieval *Logos*, elaborated by Thomas Aquinas,* was the dominant belief until the beginning of the modern age. The mechanical element of the *Logos* concept was further developed into a giant machine-like universe by Giordano Bruno†, Galileo Galilei‡ and later Isaac Newton.§ The world was understood as a clock set in motion by a prime mover, functioning according to strict laws enabling humans to know all things

---

* Thomas Aquinas (1225–1274) was an Italian Dominican friar, scholar, and theologian.

† Giordano Bruno (1548–1600) was an Italian Dominican friar, mathematician, astrologer, astronomer, and philosopher. He believed that the Earth revolved around the Sun, and the Sun was one of planets in the infinite universe. The Roman Inquisition burned him at the stake for his beliefs.

‡ Galileo Galilei (1564–1642) was an Italian mathematician, astronomer, physicist and philosopher who supported Copernicanism. He invented the telescope, military compass and discovered the phases of Venus and the four satellites of Jupiter.

§ Sir Isaac Newton (1642–1727) was an English physicist and mathematician. His major work *Philosophiae Naturalis Principia Mathematica* laid the foundations for classical mechanics. It formulated the laws of motion and universal gravitation.

past, present and future. The nineteenth century with Darwin's* theory completed the mechanistic worldview of Newton and René Descartes,† whose claim was that consciousness is the sole reality: *Cogito Ergo Sum* (I think therefore I am).

Laszlo notes that "the age of Mythos was dominated by mythical consciousness; the age of Theos by theistic consciousness; and the modern age by a mechanistically rational Logos consciousness. These mindsets were useful and functional in their time. Indeed, the reason human culture and civilization continued to exist and evolve is because more adapted forms of consciousness arose from time to time. Of course, they did not arise everywhere and in all times: countless civilizations failed to survive, victims of changing conditions to which they could not adapt. This failure is not one we can contemplate today."[121]

He explains that by the end of the twentieth century civilization had entered a phase marked by increasing unsustainability. Laszlo predicts that the years 2001–2010 will be filled with high levels of stress all around, conflicts in the political spheres, and economic instability coupled with a deteriorating climate and environment. Either humanity drifts passively or opts to take its own evolution into its own hands by adapting new values and a more evolved consciousness so that a new era can be born—a sustainable post-*Logos* civilization.

---

* Charles Robert Darwin (1809–1882) was an English geologist and naturalist. He is most famous for his contribution to the theory of the evolution of species described in *On the Origin of Species* published in 1859.

† René Descartes (1596–1650) was a French philosopher, mathematician, and writer who is considered the Father of Modern Philosophy.

The post-*Logos* civilization forgets myths that say nature is inexhaustible, nature is a giant mechanism, life is a struggle for survival, the market distributes benefits to all, and the more one consumes the better off one is. Other myths, such as "order through hierarchy," "everything is reversible, and "everyone is unique and separate," are redundant beliefs, which have outlived their usefulness. It is essential to replace these obsolete beliefs with others more in tune with the state of the world. One such belief is that it is possible to find unity within the diversity of the contemporary world. This assures a peaceful and sustainable future by means of cooperation between the world's diverse peoples and cultures. Beliefs and values are the two determining factors in how humans perceive the world, affecting human behavior both at the individual and the societal level. Laszlo suggests new values and beliefs to be embraced, accepted, and shared by humans at large—a *planetary ethic.*

"A planetary ethic respects the conditions under which all people in the world community can live in dignity and freedom, without destroying each other's chances of livelihood, culture, society, and environment."[122] What does this universal morality entail? Laszlo's response is that the planetary ethic embraces all people regardless of religion, skin color, age, and gender or secular/religious beliefs. People are free to pursue their self-interests as long as this allows others to live as well. Here "others" include all living beings including animals and plants.

Our common future depends on our accepting individual and collective responsibility in line with planetary ethics.

Personal responsibilities are no longer only a private concern. They are everybody's business, says Laszlo. The common future is determined by what each human being does and how he or she does it. Individual thinking must extend to global thinking following the rule *live in a way that allows all others to live as well.* Thinking globally and acting locally needs to be the rule followed by business; they are pivotal for the outcome of a macroshift. "The last but by no means the least of the new imperatives of our time is to accept the multiple facets of the responsibility that we must shoulder. As private individuals, we must think globally and act morally. As leaders or collaborators in business, we must care for all stakeholders and for the environment. And as citizens of our country, we must support leaders who recognize the need for locally as well as globally informed and implemented policies."[123]

HOLOS CIVILIZATION

Humanity evolved from *Mythos* to *Theos*, then from *Theos* to *Logos*. A new dawn reflects light on a new civilization governed by a new holistic rationality—the *Holos* civilization.

"Logos-inspired evolution was materialistic and conquest- and consumption-oriented. The alternative to it is evolution centered on human development and development of human communities."[124] The world at Holos is globally whole but locally diverse in essence. It denotes a world of self-reliant communities that interact and cooperate not just locally but globally. Nation-states are part of regional communities and act accordingly. They participate in a wider network of regions representing diversity for the achievement of unity. People in Holos civilization live more healthily and more simply, cap population growth and respect their environment. Holos worldview recognizes unity within social and cultural diversity with a deep sense of consciousness. It marks a progress from competition to reconciliation and partnership; from greed to sufficiency and caring; from outer to inner authority; from separation to wholeness; from mechanistic to living systems and from organizational fragmentation to coherent integration.

Is Holos civilization a utopia? Far from it, says Laszlo. He refers to Paul H. Ray and Sherry R. Anderson,* two American sociologists and researchers who carried out periodical surveys and concluded that an alternative culture is growing with progressive standards versus those with traditional and conservative levels of living. Ray and Anderson indicated that these people opt out from the establishment by striving to evolve their values and vision and change their lifestyles. They have a strong awareness of planet-wide issues such as climate change, feel a strong bond with nature, help others voluntarily, desire equality for women and men in all spheres of life, and want to create a more sustainable lifestyle. Ray and Anderson estimated that there are about fifty million so-called "cultural creative" in the United States and another eighty to ninety million in Europe.

---

* *Cultural Creatives: How 50 Million People Are Changing the World* by Paul H. Ray and Sherry Ruth Anderson, published by Harmony Books, USA, 2000.

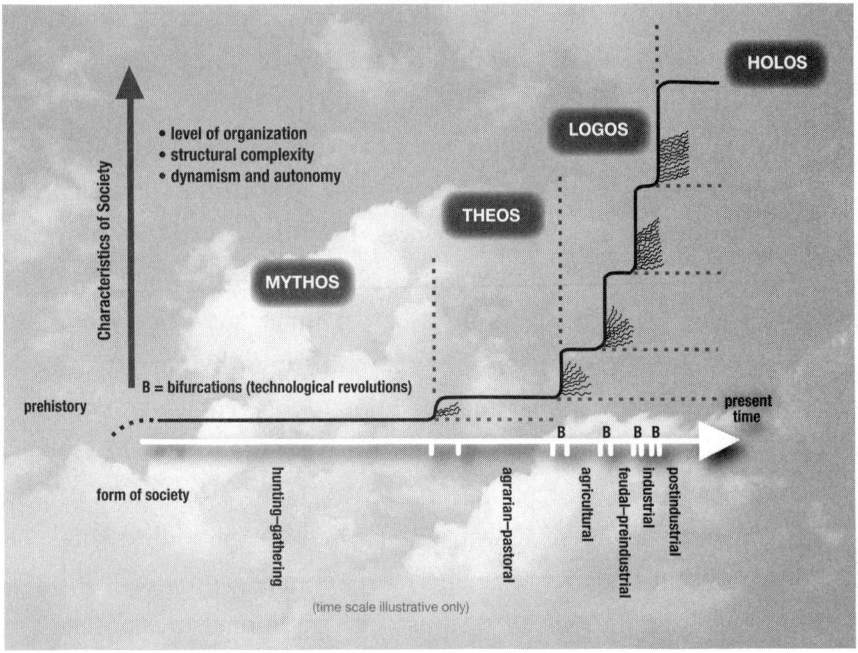

Major Stages in the Evolution of Society

(Courtesy of Ervin Laszlo)

Can One Change the World?

Cultural Creatives think and act according to global ethics; they are creating the *Holos* civilization. The crucial thing is that they evolve their consciousness. "The threat to human survival has its ultimate roots in the outdated consciousness of a critical mass in today's world. If the obsolescence of today's dominant consciousness is the root cause of the survival threat, evolution of consciousness is the way to overcome that threat. You, as everyone around you, can do your part by evolving your own consciousness."[125]

How does one evolve one's consciousness? Laszlo reminds us that the brain's two hemispheres have different functions. The left hemisphere is responsible for more rational thinking whereas the right one is more about intuitive perception. Holos consciousness is characterized by a whole-brain consciousness with both hemispheres functioning in equal measure.

"Having whole-brain Holos consciousness is not a matter of adding more facts and figures to the storehouse of facts and figures already in your head. Relevant facts and figures are important, but alone they do not fill the bill. To live with and not against each other, to live in a way that does not rob the chances of others to live as well, to care what is happening to the poor and the powerless as well as to nature calls for more than reading up on the statistics. It also calls for feeling and intuition, for sensing the situation in which we find ourselves, and for apprehending its manifold aspects and creatively responding to it. It means raising the full scope of our attention, empathy, and concern from today's ego-, business-, and nation-centered dimension to a broader human-, nature-, and planet-centered one."[126]

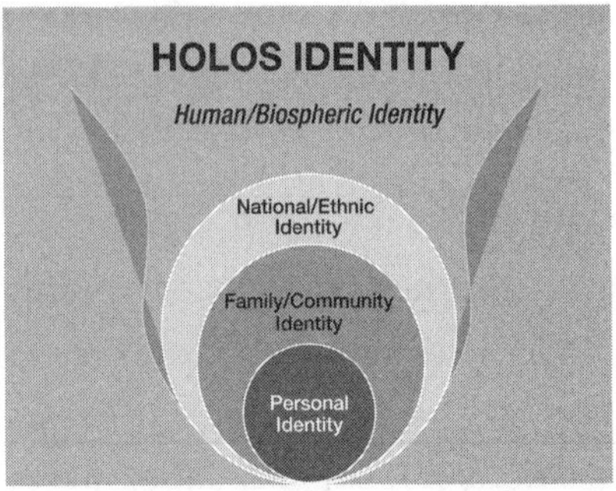

a.

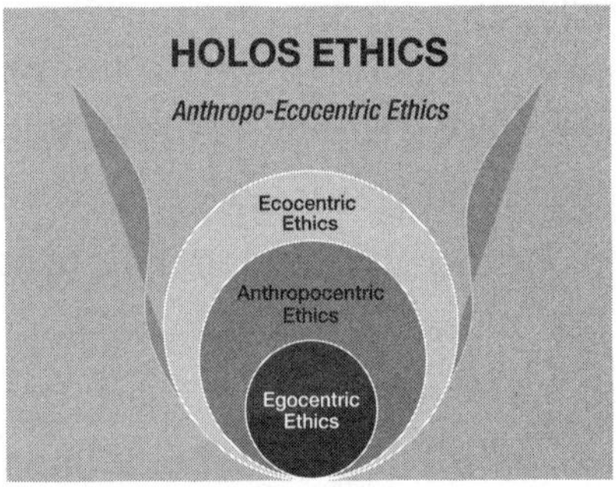

b.

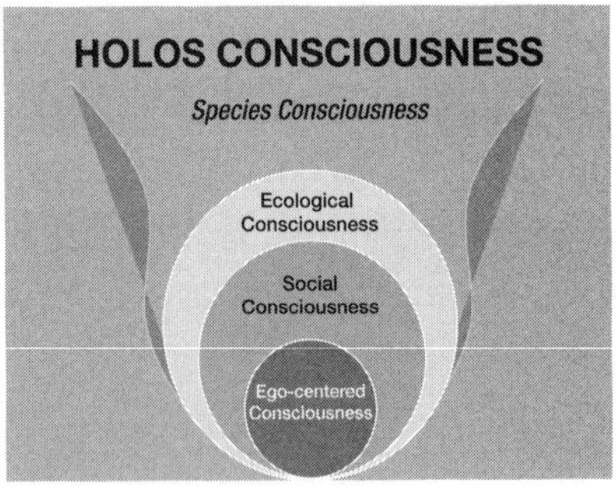

c.

Holos Identity, Holos Ethics, Holos Consciousness

(Illustrations courtesy of Ervin Laszlo)

The Manifesto of Planetary Consciousness

The following text was drafted by Ervin Laszlo in consultation with the Dalai Lama and adopted by the Club of Budapest on October 27, 1996.

A new way of thinking has become the necessary condition for responsible living and acting. Evolving means fostering creativity in all people, in all parts of the world. Creativity is not a genetic but a cultural endowment of human beings. Culture and society change fast, while genes change slowly: no more than one half of one percent of human genetic endowment is likely to alter in an entire century. Hence most of our genes date from the Stone Age or before; they cold help us to live in the jungles of nature but not in the jungles of civilization. Today's economic, social, and technological environment is our own creation, and only the creativity of our mind—our culture, spirit, and consciousness—will enable us to cope with it. Genuine creativity does not remain paralyzed when faced with unusual and unexpected problems but confronts them openly, without prejudice. Cultivating it is a precondition of finding our way toward a globally interconnected society in which individuals, enterprises, states, and the whole family of peoples and nations could live together peacefully, cooperatively, and with mutual benefit.

A Call for Responsibility

In the course of the twentieth century, people in many parts of the world have become conscious of their rights as well as of many persistent violations of them. This development is important, but in itself it is not enough. We must now become conscious of the factor without neither rights nor other values can be effectively safeguarded: our individual and collective *responsibilities*. We are not likely to grow into a peaceful and cooperative human family unless we become responsible social, economic, political, and cultural actors.

We human beings need more than food, water, and shelter; more even than remunerated work, self-esteem, and social acceptance. We also need something to live for: an ideal to achieve, a responsibility to accept. Because we are aware of the consequences of our actions, we can and must accept responsibility for them. In today's world all people, no matter where they live and what they do, have become responsible for their actions as:

- private individuals
- citizens of a country
- collaborators in business and the economy
- members of the human community
- persons endowed with mind and consciousness

As individuals, we are responsible for seeking our interests in harmony with, and not at the expense of, the interests and well-being of others; responsible for condemning and averting any form of killing and brutality; responsible for not bringing more children into the world than we truly need and can support; and for respecting the right of life, development, and equal status and dignity of all the children, women, and men who inhabit the Earth.

As citizens of our country, we are responsible for demanding that our leaders "beat swords into plowshares" and relate to other nations peacefully and in a spirit of cooperation; that they recognize the legitimate aspirations of all communities in the human family; and that they do not abuse sovereign powers to manipulate people and the environment for shortsighted and selfish ends.

As collaborators in business and actors in the economy, we are responsible for ensuring that corporate objectives do not center uniquely on profit and growth but include a concern that products and services respond to human needs and demands without harming people and impairing nature; that they do not serve destructive ends and unscrupulous designs; and that they respect the rights of all entrepreneurs and enterprises who compete fairly in the global marketplace.

As members of the human community, it is our responsibility to adopt a culture of nonviolence, solidarity, and economic, political, and social equality, promoting mutual understanding and respect among people and nations whether they are like us or different, demanding that all people everywhere should be empowered to respond to the challenges that face them with the material as well as spiritual resources that are required for this unprecedented task.

And *as persons endowed with mind and consciousness*, our responsibility is to encourage comprehension and appreciation for the excellence of the human spirit in all its manifestations, and for inspiring awe and wonder for a cosmos that brought forth life and consciousness and holds out the possibility of its continued evolution toward ever higher levels of insight, understanding, love, and compassion.

A Call for Planetary Consciousness

In most parts of the world the real potential of human beings is sadly underdeveloped. The way children are raised depresses their faculties for learning and creativity; the way young people experience the struggle for material survival results in frustration and resentment. In adults this leads to a variety of compensatory, addictive, and compulsive behaviors. The result is the persistence of social and political oppression, economic warfare, cultural intolerance, crime, and disregard for the environment.

Eliminating social and economic ills and frustrations calls for considerable socioeconomic development, and that is not possible without better education, information, and communication. These, however, are blocked by the absence of socioeconomic development, so that a vicious cycle is produced: underdevelopment creates frustration, and frustration, giving rise to defective behaviors, blocks development. This cycle must be broken at its point of greatest flexibility and that is the development of the spirit and consciousness of human beings. Achieving this objective does not preempt the need for socioeconomic development with all its financial and technical resources but calls for a parallel mission in the spiritual field. Unless people's spirit and consciousness evolve to the planetary dimension, the processes that stress the globalized society-nature system will intensify and create a shock wave that could jeopardize the entire transition toward a peaceful and cooperative global society. This would be a setback for humanity and a danger for everyone. Evolving human spirit and consciousness is the first vital cause shared by the whole of the human family.

Planetary consciousness is knowing as well as feeling the vital interdependence and essential oneness of humankind and the conscious adoption of the ethic and the ethos that this entails. Its evolution is the basic imperative of human survival on this planet. [127]

CONCLUDING REMARKS ON MACROSHIFT

The message of this book is that the world currently is experiencing a wide-range evolutionary transformation that leads toward a global shift in civilization. This shift is all-embracing, irreversible, rapid and global and affects all aspects of life. Established values, vision and behaviors have to be reviewed because they are essential parts of a system that is dysfunctional. Humans must update the way they perceive the world, and the way they value it in order to change the way they act in it.

Laszlo outlines in this book two possible scenarios. The "Breakdown" option where humanity chooses to remain passive and let chaos, destruction and anarchy occur. The "Breakthrough" option, by contrast, entails an important individual and collective transformation in thinking and behavior to generate innovative solutions to the global problems. He states that each human being is capable of such change; the power is in everybody's hands. Laszlo presents a higher plane on which a global perspective emerges. In his view the single most important factor for change is a mass awakening and realization of global consciousness. More precisely, Laszlo's real message is that we need to evolve a global consciousness.

CHAPTER 11

The Relevance and Application of the Cosmic Information Field Theory to the Problems of Our Times

Macroshift Means Globalshift

Laszlo published *Quantum Shift in the Global Brain, How the New Scientific Reality Can Change Us and Our World* in 2008. Macroshift in society, paradigm shift in science, and globalshift in action are its main themes. What does he mean by the title of the book? Laszlo states "The global brain is the quasi-neural energy- and information processing network created by six and a half billion humans on the planet, interacting in many ways, private as well as public, and on many levels, local as well as global. A quantum shift in the global brain is a sudden and fundamental transformation in the relations of a significant segment of the six and a half billion humans to each other and to nature—*a macroshift society*—and a likewise sudden and fundamental transformation in cutting-edge perceptions regarding the nature of reality—*a paradigm shift in science*. The two shifts together make for a veritable 'reality revolution' in society as well as in science."[128]

He claims change is apparent everywhere; it is no longer merely a theory. Climate, ecology, economics, society, politics, science, and cultural and personal transformations represent reality in a state of flux. A passive attitude, business as usual, and hoping for miracles are no longer an option. The survival of human civilization and our planet calls for the co-creation of a new paradigm, which is based on close connection to each other and to the cosmos. Evolution or extinction: This is the primary question we face in the twenty first century.

Laszlo repeatedly emphasizes that humankind has a choice. But is it too late to change? Has the planet reached a tipping point where the smallest attractor can trigger rapid, catastrophic events? In Laszlo's view, nature—a dynamic system—is as capable of rapid transformation as humanity itself. "When such a system nears the point where the existing structures and feedbacks can no longer maintain its integrity, it becomes ultrasensitive and responds even to the smallest provocation for change. In this state 'butterfly effects' are possible. In today's near-chaotic, unstable, and hence ultrasensitive world such 'butterflies' as the thinking, the values, the ethic, and the consciousness of a critical mass in society can trigger fundamental transformation."[129]

Tipping points—Macroshifts—impact every aspect and spectrum of society; no societal segment is left unaffected.

Previous Macroshifts were local or regional, whereas now Macroshift is global and humanity's societal evolution involves the whole planet. The current global tipping point (bifurcation point) and the possible directions for humankind (the breakdown or the breakthrough) are represented in Laszlo's image below.

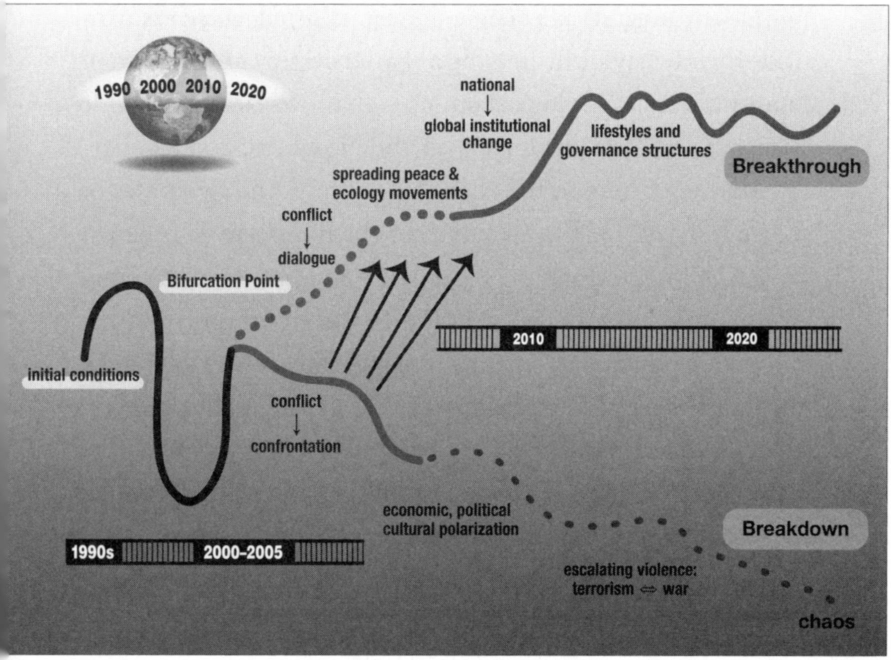

Bifurcation Point, Breakdown and Breakthrough of Humankind

(Illustration courtesy of Ervin Laszlo)

Laszlo continually repeats that human consciousness can influence the outcome of this bifurcation. "Humans will and purpose decide whether the world heads toward breakdown or toward breakthrough. This sensitivity to human intervention is a remarkable feature of today's civilization. It places a unique opportunity in our hands: the opportunity to tip the scales of human destiny."[130]

Laszlo suggests all people adhere to a *planetary ethic*, to guide their behavior in creating a shared destiny for the human community. An "Ecological ethic" is characterized by an ethic of sustainable human impact on the biosphere, and the harmonization of human life with the rhythms and dynamics of nature in order for the evolution of the biosphere to progress flawlessly. Maintaining the biosphere's equilibrium and transforming humankind's relationship to the environment at the individual, national and global levels are the keys to long-term sustainability. To ensure that all people share equally the planet's resources, there is a need to establish a code of planetary ethic, which "asks people to respect the conditions under which all people can live. The indicated minimum code is: *Live so that others can also live.*"[131]

Laszlo is convinced that the transformation of the human species has already begun. More and more people recognize that if the human race's current lifestyles remain unchanged, it will eventually lead to the extinction of humankind. Cultural Creatives are the torchbearers for shifting away from a fragmented, egotistic civilization toward a co-creative, cooperative world. The time to act is now and act consciously according to the new understanding of the world outlined by science. "Quantum shift in the global brain embraces both our experience and our understanding of the world. Not only is the world around us in radical transformation, but also our understanding of the fundamental nature of the world—and of the universe itself—is shifting. This is important, for our world is an integral part of the universe; its laws and processes apply on Earth the same as everywhere else. A sound orientation in our world calls for a sound understanding of the universe."[132]

Laszlo's profound cosmic plenum, the theory of a nonlocally interconnected field, offers a comprehensive framework to reach new understanding about the nature of humankind and the cosmos. The Akashic field *underlies* all the manifest phenomena of the cosmos and at the same time it *becomes* all the manifest phenomena. The Akashic field is the foreground and background of everything, the cradle and burying ground of all, the cyclic beginning and end of all universes.

The rediscovery of this concept offers a new understanding, not just about the nature of humankind and the cosmos, but also a new perspective on why and how humans use their privileged capacity for consciousness. "The rapid spread of an evolved consciousness is crucial for humanity's future. Whether such consciousness reaches a critical mass will decide if humanity moves in time from the business as usual scenario leading to breakdown to the transformation scenario that leads toward a new civilization."[133]

What happens if there are not enough people with evolved consciousness to achieve a fundamental shift in global values, morals, and behavior? How can only a relatively small number of people instigate change by empowering political leaders who favor economic cooperation, intercultural solidarity, and ecological responsibility; and businesses leaders who choose the collective gain instead of the pursuit of pure profit? Does the world have to wait for global catastrophes to trigger global cooperation? Laszlo believes that human consciousness can evolve and already does so at the frontiers of society. He says that "quantum shift in the global brain is humanity's best chance. Margaret Mead said, 'Never doubt the power of a small group of people to change the world. Nothing else ever has.' Small groups of people with an evolved consciousness will change the world—if they grow into a critical mass in time."[134]

In the chapter "GlobalShift in Action," Laszlo presents the *Manifesto on Planetary Consciousness* that he drafted with His Holiness the 14th Dalai Lama in 1996, and discusses the aims and objectives of the World Wisdom Council, which he has been closely involved with through the Club of Budapest organization.

In the very last chapter of his book, "Explores an Explanation," Laszlo for the first time makes public a personal experience, a communication he received from beyond the grave via instrumental transcommunication (ITC). He explores an explanation of his paranormal experience in the light of Akashic theory. Laszlo stated many times before that the universe is fundamentally and nonlocally coherent. Nonlocal coherence between the minds of individuals is mediated by their brains and bodies and thus accounts for phenomena like telepathy, remote viewing, remote healing, twin pain, and so on. What happens if there is no brain or body associated with mind? Can communication still occur between the living and the non-living?

The growing number of experiments and experiences in the field of ITC presents another anomaly that mainstream science so far cannot find explanation for. Hoaxes are always possible, yet Laszlo had no doubt that what he experienced was real, not fake. He was invited to psychic researcher, Marcello Bacci's group meeting in Italy, where he demonstrated how "for the past forty years he has been hearing voices through his radio and has become convinced that they are the voices of people who have passed away. Those who come to his regular 'dialogues with the dead' are likewise convinced of this. They are people who have lost a son or a daughter, a father or mother or a spouse, and hope to have the experience of hearing them talk through Bacci's radio."[135]

Laszlo did not communicate with any of his lost family members, but he conversed with someone or something speaking in clear Hungarian without accent. The session was recorded on both audio and film formats. Over several decades, a number of physicists and electronic engineers have tested Bacci's sessions utilizing ultra-fine measurements and devices, and none has found any trickery involved. Mainstream science finds ITC experiments like Bacci's clearly perplexing and anomalous. How does Laszlo explain his paranormal experience?

"No doubt, from a deeper spiritual and human point of view, the ITC phenomenon is extraordinarily important;

it merits serious investigation in regard to the feasibility of finding a scientifically acceptable explanation. This requires connecting the phenomenon of transcommunication with an independently developed theory of the nature of consciousness and the possibility of its persistence following the deactivation of the brain with which it was associated. The theory of the information-recording, conserving, and transmitting of cosmic plenum is a promising candidate for his research."[136] In his view, instrumental transcommunication is "a natural process mediated by the Akashic field (A-field) of the cosmic plenum. In connecting the ITC phenomenon with the theory of the A-field, the key principle is the transfer of information between holograms—in this case, between holograms generated by interfering wave fronts in the cosmic plenum."[137] Transcommunication occurs when the resonance of the holographic lifetime information trace left in the A-field by the deceased person meshes with the resonance of the hologram created by the brain of the living interlocutor.

Instrumental transcommunication is one of many modes via which the conserved information in the cosmic plenum becomes accessible. "The logical place to seek a scientific explanation for the mystery of transcommunication is not the metaphysics of souls and spirits but the physics of complex field theory."[138]

Laszlo's *Quantum Shift in the Global Brain* promotes a progressive shift from scientific materialism to a multidimensional worldview in unison with the world's spiritual traditions. Laszlo emphasizes that humanity is at a crossroads where it can choose between being the last decade of a vanishing, obsolete world or the first of a new one. In these books in particular, he focuses on the problems, opportunities, and challenges humanity faces, both individually and collectively. In parallel with these pragmatic issues, he argues that the latest developments in science are creating fertile ground for a global shift.

Humans can be willfully constructive or destructive. The latter attitude stems from an incorrect worldview, one seeing humans as distinctly independent entities, passive agents unable to direct the course of their lives. A more constructive worldview sees humankind as an integral and coherent agent, intrinsically and subtly interconnected with the cosmos. Holding such a holistic worldview encourages individuals to make conscious life choices, which recognize and foster harmony between the mental and physical spheres, as well as between community and environment.

In the Appendix to *WorldShift 2012*, Laszlo issued a declaration, a global wake-up call, which was also circulated on various websites such those of the WorldShift 2012,* WorldShift Movement,† WorldShift International‡ (these were initiated by Ervin Laszlo and co-founded with Gyorgyi Szabo) and partner organizations:

* WorldShift 2012 – http://worldshift2012.org.

† WorldShift Movement – http://www.worldshiftmovement.org.

‡ WorldShift International – http://www.worldshiftinternational.org.

The State of Global Emergency

There is no doubt that we are now in a state of global emergency. This unprecedented worldwide crisis is a symptom of a much deeper problem: the current state of our consciousness—how we think about ourselves and our world. We have the urgent need, and now the opportunity, for a complete rethink: to consider our values and priorities, to understand our interconnectedness, and to shift in a new direction, living in harmony with nature and each other.

Every person, community, and society in the world is already, or will soon be, affected by the global crisis, through climate change, economic breakdown, ecosystem collapse, population pressure, food and water shortages, resource depletion, and nuclear and other threats. If we continue on our present unsustainable path, by mid-century the Earth could become largely uninhabitable for human and countless other life forms. However, total-system collapse caused by ecocatastrophes or escalating wars triggered by religious, geopolitical, or resource conflicts could occur much sooner.

These threats are real. The underlying causes of the present global crisis have been building momentum for decades and could soon become irreversible. Estimates of when the point of no return will be reached have been reduced from the end of the century, to mid-century, to the next twenty years, and recently to the next five to then years.

The WorldShift 2012 Declaration

The window of opportunity for pulling out of the current crisis and breaking through to a peaceful and sustainable world may be no more than a few years from now. This timeline coincides with the many forecasts and prophecies that speak of the end of the current cycle of human life on this planet and the possible dawning of a new consciousness by the end of the year 2012.

Today millions of forward-thinking groups and individuals all over the world are addressing the many opportunities presented at this critical time. Designs for sustainable systems, structures, and technologies are being developed and implemented in all sectors, at all levels, and in every society. This global awakening is a hopeful sign of the vitality of the human spirit and our ability to the dangers we now face with insight and creativity.

The Crisis and the Opportunity

The totality of our current efforts does not yet match the scope, scale, and urgency of the necessary transformation. If we now collaborate and act with vision, foresight, and commitment we can lay the foundation for a global community that is both peaceful and sustainable. We may then ensure our survival and well-being as well as that of future generations. While the window of time is still open, our top priority as global citizens is to accelerate our evolutionary shift to a planetary consciousness and, together, build a peaceful, just and sustainable world.

An Urgent Call

We accordingly issue this urgent call to all peoples of the world to deepen our awareness of both the dangers and the opportunities of the global crisis. We declare our firm commitment to work together to bring about a timely and positive WorldShift for the survival and well-being of all the peoples of the human community and the flourishing of all life on Earth.

Laszlo's prolific work is not limited to publishing his theories and ideas but actively promoting them by calling together thought-leaders, social activists, politicians, business and spiritual leaders to instigate worldshift. Apart from establishing the Club of Budapest Foundation in 1993, he initiated numerous organizations whose members are dedicated to carry out conscious change in the world. Besides the above-mentioned WorldShift 2012, WorldShift Movement, WorldShift International organizations, Laszlo founded *Worldshift 20 Council,* which formulated and globally circulated the following manifesto.

WorldShift 20 Declaration

Issued by the WorldShift 20 Council, November 8, 2010
An Initiative of the Club of Budapest

The Mission of the WorldShift 20 Council

The WorldShift 20 Council is composed of twenty prominent global citizens from diverse cultures and religions worldwide. The mission of the Council is to give urgent attention to the new condition of the world emerging today and provide essential orientation so that an informed and determined movement toward a peaceful and sustainable planetary civilization could be brought into being.

The Council's mission is to articulate the collective voice of humanity, drawing on the heritage of all peoples, cultures and religions. It is to transcend short-term and self-serving economic and political interests in recognition of the fact that thinking and acting in exclusive reference to narrow national or multi-national agendas cannot solve the problems currently confronting humanity. The pursuit of narrow interests are accelerating systemic breakdown in our presently unsustainable world.

The WS20 Council intends to shift the attention of the global public and media from the increasingly intractable problems and deepening crises of our deteriorating world to the opportunities and vistas of a new world where seven billion and more human beings can live in peace, prosperity and harmony with each other and the Earth's natural systems.

The WS20 Declaration

BASIC PREMISES

On-going efforts by the leaders of the industrialized states to re-adjust the collapsing systems of our unsustainable world are far from a sufficient response to the current crisis. Systemic collapse cannot be either wished away or ignored. Current global systems of economics, governance, societal organization and ecological relationships between humanity and nature must be urgently re-designed based on the consciousness, values and principles which can provide peace and long-term sustainability for the human community. The "window of opportunity" to begin such a large-scale transition may only remain open for a few years from now.

However, the international community is the prisoner of '*silo thinking*' in meetings such as those of the G20. Negotiators from leading economies build upon narrowly specialized agendas inherited from the past; acting in the name of creating more economic growth to make narrowly defined economic coordination problems more negotiable. This kind of thinking was evident in the G20's Seoul Summit. The Declaration issuing from that Summit reads like an emergency report of Ministers of Trade and Finance, rather than a report on the deliberations on the wellbeing of the world community of the heads of government of the world's twenty most powerful nations. International trade disequilibria, discriminating exchange rate policies, and the threat of recurring financial crises occupied center stage, with scant attention to climate change, the global ecology, and the endemic poverty of nearly one half of the world's peoples—and no attention whatsoever to the wealth, power, and consumption orientation that dominates the aspirations of the world's influential governments, businesses, and populations.

The Seoul Summit Document agreed by the leaders presents an Action Plan that provides a clear illustration of the narrow and short-term vision of the world's political leaders. The Action Plan centers on five policy areas listed in the following order: monetary and exchange rate policies, trade and development policies, fiscal policies, financial reforms, and structural reforms. The range of the latter is limited to the objective to "boost and sustain global demand, foster job creation, contribute to global rebalancing, and increase our [the G20's] growth potential." Yet even these measures of structural reform could hardly have inspired the confidence of the leaders themselves, as at the conclusion of the Summit the President of the United States felt compelled to go on television to address a plea to the trade surplus nations to voluntarily limit their exports to the United States.

A focus on short-term economic and financial issues is crisis management, and not an acceptable response by the world's political leaders to humanity's intensifying problems. The kind of economic growth that the G20 treats as a panacea is merely a bolstering of the same unsustainable economic system that is threatening the wellbeing and even the survival of vast underprivileged populations, and is altering the planet's climate and damaging its ecologies. Today's looming climate, ecology, energy and nuclear threats are neither manageable by purely economic and fiscal measures, nor isolable into narrow specialty areas.

The human community needs thoroughgoing structural reform so that our children and grandchildren may live in peace with one another and with the ecological systems that sustain human life and existence. We need to redesign our societies so that they become *ecologically and energetically viable. And we need to address the major twin threats to humanity's continuing survival: global warming, and nuclear weapons.*

If unstopped, the climatic changes produced by global warming will come together with such profound synergies that no human power will be sufficient to retain them. They will inexorably synergize in spontaneous interactions and disastrous effects until, in the next 100 years, more than 80 percent of the human species would have perished due to climate-induced catastrophes, epidemics of diseases sweeping into new terrains, and human conflict and war as a result of the most massive migration of peoples in human history—hundreds of millions, even billions of climatic refugees moving across the continents. This prediction, made among others by pioneering biologist James Lovelock, merits sober and clear consideration.

The abolition of nuclear weapons, in turn, is no longer merely a lofty goal and noble aspiration: it is essential for human survival. Peace is impossible as long as the threat of nuclear war hangs over our heads. A Nuclear Weapons Convention prohibiting the production as well as the use of all nuclear weapons in all circumstances is urgently needed. In a democratic world, such a Convention must be constructed by awakening the public to the threat of maintaining vast arsenals of weapons that could destroy all life on Earth. Such an awakening is already in progress. In 21 countries, including the five major nuclear powers, polls show that 76 percent of people support negotiation of a treaty banning all nuclear weapons.

But opposition is still strong. Nuclear weapons are about power, and governments have not given up what they perceive as a source of their power. Powerful military-industrial complexes are trading on a fear that has been purposively foisted on the public. In the mainstream media there is a virtual blackout on this subject, and this makes it difficult to bring about the consensus needed to democratically initiate measures that could eliminate the nuclear sword of Damocles that is now hanging over our heads.

An Alternative Philosophy

A Conscious Leadership

There is no longer any time to waste if civilization on this planet is to endure and prosper. It is the responsibility of the people to choose leadership that is knowledgeable and wise, and the responsibility of the leadership to move forward in ways that preserve the viability of the social structure into the future by respecting appropriate global principles.

Conscious leadership is called for by those in positions of decision-taking at every level of society today. National political leaders need the ability to bring what are seen as oppositional forces into collaboration; promoting new skills that can match our inner capacities to the outer complexities of life and integral solutions that honor psychological, biological, social, cultural and environmental dimensions so as to navigate the changes that are upon us; developing new skills, including cultural competencies, social and emotional intelligence that can make it possible to work well together.

We now have the capacities to create integrated planning processes that can lead to new perspectives on every aspect of human endeavor. A global system of enterprise can invite creative breakthroughs. A fresh new approach to governance can invite greater participation from all segments of society. An interconnected web of global commerce can be grounded in a set of priorities that allow for competition in the embrace of cooperation. Business can flourish by putting people first, designing systems of global synergy that can move our world's cultures to new levels of prosperity. Through conscious leadership, we can encompass individual and global needs as an interrelated, interdependent whole.

The leaders of the developed countries need to ask a paramount question: What good is it to be rich in a sick world? Having done the most to increase their wealth at the expense of a depleted planet, the leaders of the G20 should focus on bringing about a well planet for coming generations. Economies everywhere need to be peaceful, fair, sustainable, and healthy on all levels. With global wellness in mind, we can unite to bring the ecology back into balance, eradicate pandemic disease, lift up the dispossessed, and curb military aggression.

Only global thinking can accomplish these ends, but to date the lingering effects of nationalism and tribalism block real progress. Nonetheless, even if we cannot yet think of ourselves as one people, we can agree that we live on one planet. A sick planet is just a few steps away from a dying planet. Once that truth sinks in, effective programs for global wellness have a chance. We may be able to survive in a drastically depleted world, but we cannot be fully human in such a world.

A New Consciousness

We need to leave everything we know behind in order to get to where we need to go. This might seem counterintuitive but it is actually essential, given Einstein's observation that the consciousness that produced the problem cannot get us out of it; only a new consciousness can. This means that there must be a systemic thorough reinvention of every aspect of humanity—the birth of a new consciousness.

There are many crises affecting humanity and many others are yet to come. All these crises are effects of the same cause: the lack of a "planetary consciousness." We lack a holistic perspective that embraces both humankind and the ecosystem. In a democracy the majority rules, decides and imposes its laws and behaviour, and people with a planetary consciousness are still in the minority.

We need a consciousness that recognizes that wide-ranging cooperation based on solidarity and oriented toward fundamental transformation is the basic precondition for human peace and sustainability. We need a consciousness that inspires and motivates cooperation not only in the economic and financial domain, but also in the domain of the ecology, as well as in technology, education, public information, and cultural communication. We need a planetary consciousness that unambiguously apprehends the interdependence and the Oneness of all People on Earth, and the Oneness of our destiny.

The leaders of the G20 did not create the world's problems but perpetuate them by basing their interactions on a limited and narrow level of consciousness. A lack of gratitude toward the environment, exploitive treatment of animal life, plant life and the world of nature, discrimination against people, cultures, and nations—these kinds of destructive behaviors do not originate solely from the minds of a small group of leaders. They also arise from the consciousness of billions of individual human beings. We must support the efforts of each global citizen, whether in a leadership role or not, to take responsibility for uplifting their consciousness thereby safeguarding the future of our human society and the Earth.

Reorientation in the Public Sector

Since the publication of the *Limits to Growth* in 1972 many events and movements have rung the alarm bell in the world loud and clear, yet the situation of the planet has not changed for the better. We know that many authoritative international organizations, such as the United Nations and the G20, have made efforts for bringing about change, and that countless NGOs and grassroots groups have done so as well. However, these efforts have been fragmented and have not been implemented quickly and effectively enough. A Concrete Action Plan is urgently needed for the passengers on Spaceship Earth for spreading and sharing planetary consciousness, and thereby producing the foundations for a new way of living and acting in society.

We need to replace the obsolete notions of nation-states, where national governments are in charge of ensuring the national interest, which they conceive as achieving the objective of bringing about "recovery," "renewed stability" and "balanced growth" in their own economy. Instead of attempts to re-vitalize the current intrinsically unsustainable and terminally crisis-bound system, a thorough transformation of current structures and practices is required.

We need a new social function based on partnership between Governments, NGOs and Civil Society to connect and communicate "breakthroughs" wherever they occur in the global community. The requirement is for a new function to enhance social synergy and cooperation of all that is creative and emergent leading and able to motivate a whole-system shift. Through the Internet we can scan for, map, connect and communicate what is working in the world, country by country and community by community.

The debacle of Copenhagen last December demonstrated the inability of intergovernmental organizations to transcend national and corporate interests and deal objectively with critical global issues. This tragic failure was due to a lack of understanding that the global crisis is actually a whole-system crisis of the human spirit. By ignoring the spiritual dimension of human reality and continuing to reduce everything to economics, the world will only spiral toward greater and greater catastrophes. The G20 perpetuates this failure of perspective. We are at a point in time when the spiritual dimension must become paramount in issues of decision making. World leaders should be committed in their decision-making processes to spiritual principles higher than monetary politics, and to the realization that the planet is a whole system and that, therefore, all decisions for the global good must be made on that basis lest the human species forfeit its future.

It is fundamental for leaders to encourage widespread support for the discovery of a deeper meaning of life, an inner joy that is not dependent on circumstances and a compassion that leads to care for other beings. We need to co-create a world in which we can live together free from unnecessary fear and in harmony with our surroundings based on a collective awakening, and governed by wisdom and compassion rather than by greed and fear.

Governments need to consider whether the entire concept of spirituality needs to be rearticulated in the light of a global society. Spirituality cuts across barriers of race and religion, sex and nationality, and is therefore best suited for a global community. We need to re-articulate certain universal concepts that will enable us to cope with the challenges and hazards of globalization. Many of these concepts are in the great religious traditions of humanity. They need to be rediscovered and reaffirmed in the context of the contemporary world.

URGENT INSTITUTIONAL STEPS

Nation-States must work together to address critical challenges. All states state should establish an office for the specific fulfillment of the Millennium Development Goals and establish a regular reporting system on the progress of each state's plan to fulfill its Millennium Development Goal commitments. Capital is a means to that end, not an end in itself. Capital must be protected as other property rights, but not in derogation of adverse impacts on the rights of individual people and biological systems that have existential value beyond the market. Life itself must be understood as sacred and revered.

A new bottom line must be established which incorporates the well-being of the environment and of people as part of the social bargain of society as a limited liability entity. We must implement a proper valuation of the natural world independent of human interests at all levels of wealth measurement. National sovereignty must be balanced with universal norms and values based on principles of harmony with nature, identification of shared interests in peace amongst states, and the rule of law.

We must restore the primacy of the People and of collective values to guide humanity's common destiny. An important step in this direction would be to re-adopt in the 21st Century the 20th Century's Universal Declaration of Human Rights.

We need to create a Social Harmony Index in every nation of the world. It is to consist of an environmental index, armament index, human rights index, honesty index, freedom index, democracy index, free flowing information index, government public affairs index, public security index, rich poor gap index, urban rural index, education popularization index, national physical condition index, creative ability index, social security index, as well as others. By integrating these data over decades we get the Social Harmony Index (SHI), a composite evaluation of every society and its rating in the world. By integrating the SHI of all countries, we get the World Social Harmony Index (WSHI) and can perceive its pattern of change year by year. These indices need to be evaluated, integrated and re-issued every year by a special organization attached to the United Nations or to the G20. They will serve as a frame of reference for every country's development and by spurring the rectification of deviations, enhance the impact of public opinion on the government. Every Nation should now be looking to intensify SHI competition and weaken GDP competition in the world.

Everyone benefits from healthy eco-systems, financially sound institutions, and thriving human communities. Thus rethinking the design assumptions of the regulatory framework of capital markets and rebuilding trust is an urgent global priority. Principles to be urgently implemented include:

- democratizing finance and widening the debate on reform by including all stakeholders and the innovations of experts and groups advocating deeper re-structuring and reforms;
- reframing global finance as a commons;
- economic theory informed by breakthroughs in a wide range of social and biological sciences;
- a commons approach where markets, as tools, can be designed to allocate indivisible "non-rival" public goods and infrastructures for equitable access and opportunities for human development.
- drawing attention to the many innovations that serve our common needs in stabilizing climate and creating equitable tools;
- energy solutions may not be in the new production of renewable energy. They may come from research on energy efficiency. This could

allow us to avoid the production of nuclear energy, to eliminate energy from coal and other non-renewable sources, and the need for production of new energy;

- creating a vision of the world in which the financial system serves a flourishing and sustainable human future.

We must make sure that the interdependence of financial markets, which impact Wall Street and Main Street and cause many people to live on No Street, become just, equitable, stable and sustainable. In this context we need to shift to a more mature "invisible" form of capitalism. This means shifting:

- from an Operational Economy based on the concept of mechanical systems to a Complexity Economy based on living systems;
- from a Knowledge Economy based on visible capital to an Empathy Economy based on invisible capital generated by trust and empathy among people with an awareness of invisible "trade-offs" between present and future generations;
- from a Monetary Economy to a Voluntary Economy as the chief economic principle;
- from a Beneficiary Economy to a Participatory Economy reflecting the real needs of citizens;

and

- from the illusion of an Unlimited Growth Economy to the shared reality of a Global Environment Economy.

Taking a whole system approach for this, the most critical time in human history, the decisions we make over the next few years will determine whether we grow or die, whether the 13.8 billion year experiment that resulted in our lives will end within the next century or two. What the world so desperately needs at this time is patterns for peaceful, passionately creative and effective societies. And with it peaceful, passionately creative and effective people—in other words the possible human in the possible society. In other words, the growth of consciousness as the paramount key to the necessary transition to a world that works for everyone and most particularly for the Planet.

We are called to take initiatives that until recently would have seemed unlikely, if not downright impossible. But now the world has been rearranged, the reset button has been hit. We no longer have the luxury of sloth or continuing in the same world destructive patterns. We must now become stewards of the planet filled with enough passion for the possible to partner one another through the greatest social transformation ever known.

We glimpse in this new century, the coming of a Planetary Society, which heralds the end of ancient and modern enmities (including that towards Nature) and the birth of new ways of using and honoring our common Humanity and its various cultures. In fact, we need a gathering of the potentials of the whole human race and the particular genius of every culture if we are going to survive our time.

This is a tremendous change, and once it is in full flower, the world will have turned a corner. Sadly today, however, we have a situation where culture has become a satellite to economics instead of economics being a satellite to culture; where the economic and governance systems we have designed and implemented are effectively blocking our collective creative potential and the possibilities for the needed transformation; where national leaders remain the gatekeepers of the old and disintegrating rather than collaborative pioneers of the new and transformative.

For the first time in human history, planetary consciousness, world peace and global sustainability are attainable goals. There are more women now in decision-making positions, and non-physical participation is made possible by the modern technologies of communication. All together, we can now create the world of which we dream.

CHAPTER 12

Akashic Philosophy: The Wider Perspectives of the New Paradigm

The Akashic Philosophy of Science

Laszlo's bold new perspective, the Akasha Paradigm, is the chrysalis of his fifty years of searching for a comprehensive understanding and description of the nature of reality and, consequently, an integral theory of everything. The Akasha Paradigm is a unity paradigm. It posits a definitive theory embracing the cutting-edge findings in physics, biology, and consciousness research, as well as bridging modern science, religion, and spirituality while providing life-sustaining implications for humankind. Since publishing *Science and the Akashic Field*, Laszlo's philosophy has matured, and he continues to work on refining and crystalizing his integral theory of everything.

The Akasha Paradigm in Science: (R)Evolution at the Cutting Edge (2012)* primarily addresses the scientific community.

* *The Akasha Paradigm in Science: (R)Evolution at the Cutting Edge* was revised and re-published with the title *The Akasha Paradigm: Revolution in Science and Evolution in Consciousness* and is currently available.

In his view, science evolves in a nonlinear fashion, punctuated by radical paradigm shifts, which are characterized as a revolutionary form of evolution—a (r)evolution. Laszlo says that 'the next (r)evolution promises to be encompassing again: shifting from the still dominant local-state paradigm to a paradigm of embracing wholeness in nature, with important implications for human life and aspiration."[139] His argument for an Akashic (R)Evolution is reinforced by four physics-oriented hypotheses in the Annexes of that book.

At the time of Laszlo's completing the manuscript of *The Akasha Paradigm Science: (R)Evolution at the Cutting Edge,* I conducted the following interview* with Ervin Laszlo in connection with this book.

INTERVIEW WITH ERVIN LASZLO

Exploring the Akasha

GYORGYI SZABO (GS): In your new book, *The Akasha Paradigm in Science: (R)evolution at the Cutting,* you take a strong scientific approach. Why did you focus your attention on explaining this particular concept—the Akasha paradigm—predominantly scientifically?

ERVIN LASZLO (EL): I want to give credibility to this concept in today's world; science means scientific, and being accepted as scientific is the mark of credibility. It is important to give credibility

* This interview appears in *The World According to Laszlo, Ervin, Portrait of a Universal Man* by Gyorgyi Szabo, published in 2016 by Ariane Publishing, Canada. The publisher granted reprint of this interview.

because the impact of the new paradigm depends on people taking it seriously. If they don't, they will ignore it. So it's important to provide a *handle* for people. Best is when they say "aha I had intuitions or experiences like that but I didn't think it was anything real. So now I see there is something to it, it has a scientific basis and I will pay more attention to it." That is the basic objective of my book. Written for scientists, but not only for scientists—for everybody who is interested in looking deeper into the question of what can we truly understand about the nature of reality.

GS: How and in what way is this book different from *Science and the Akashic Field* and your other books on the Akashic field?

EL: I published nine full-length books on the topic of an Akashic field before this one. First I called the field "psi field" (meaning by psi both the unexplained psi-phenomena and the symbol for Schrodinger's wavefunction) and then I called it the QVI (quantum vacuum interaction) field. They are all the same concept. I was searching for an explanation of a specific phenomenon: nonlocality in space and time. The idea is that the information that is the trace of all things in space and time is preserved; it does not vanish completely. It is recallable. Whatever happens to one thing at one point in space and in time happens in some subtle way to other points to other things in space in time because nothing is completely separate from any other thing. And the trace of all that is happening is preserved over time. I tried to document this and find a scientific explanation for it in terms of a field.

I have been working on the theory of such a field since the mid-eighties but the last year I realized that what we are dealing with is not just another field. This is a matrix, a unified background for all phenomena. It functions (metaphorically) as the software of the universe. The particles and systems and their interactions are the hardware, what directs or guides or governs—in the cybernetic sense—what happens to the hardware is the software. The software is the universe's "veiled dimension." It is not just a specific field. It is the fundamental dimension that manifests many different kinds of fields, such as the fields that produce electromagnetic phenomena, gravitation, and attraction and repulsion among nuclear particles. The veiled dimension also manifests the field that creates connection among phenomena and preserves their trace. These are all particular manifestations of the basic matrix that underlies all things in the universe.

GS: Let's talk about the concept of a 'field' in relation to the Akasha. Would you regard, for example, the morphic field, the zero-point field, the gravitational field, the electromagnetic field and other fields as building blocks of the Akasha? Do you see these fields as explanation and/or interpretation of specific phenomena?

EL: I call the specific fields manifestations of the Akasha. The Akasha is a multi-faceted dimension, it appears to us through its effects. Its effects include gravitation, electromagnetic phenomena, attraction and repulsion among nuclear particles, and also nonlocal connection among systems and the preservation of the trace of their interaction. These are all manifestations, manifest effects of the field.

The Akasha is prior to its manifestations: it was there before this universe was born. Our own universe came into being informed by the Akasha; the laws of nature were given already at the moment of the Big Bang. Otherwise we can't explain how this universe would be capable of giving rise to complex systems such as living organisms. For this its elements have to be amazingly well coordinated—and this can't be merely chance. According to quantum theories some ten on the five hundred is the number of the universes that would be possible. According to Penrose's calculations the possible number of universes is an even greater number. It is not plausible that our universe would have been randomly selected from this enormous number of possible universes.

GS: Einstein said: "Take all the observed facts and find the simplest scheme that can tie them all together." Is the Akasha Paradigm the simplest possible scheme that can do this?

EL: According to Einstein, the aim of science is to take into account the observed facts and find the simplest possible schema that can tie them together. The simplest possible scheme is a cosmic matrix that is "veiled" in the universe—it is not available to direct observation. The idea of this basic matrix, like all the key concepts of our thinking about the nature of reality, is freely invented. But not "anything goes." Our idea is to be tested by attempting to deduce from it the phenomena we do observe and their interrelations. A cosmic matrix that generates and interconnects all phenomena is, in my opinion, the correct idea. It is the simplest possible scheme that can tie together the facts—including the anomalous facts of nonlocality and coherence in nature.

GS: I understand that you studied extensively the works of Ludwig von Bertalanffy and Alfred North Whitehead and that that research helped you to develop the evolutionary systems theory you call the GET: General Evolution Theory. Would you say that the Akasha Paradigm can be explained in the context of a systems theory?

EL: I call the things that arise in nature "natural systems," and the things that evolve in nature "evolutionary natural systems." These systems are not something absolute and separate—they are sets of interpenetrating "stationary waves" that appear to us as material.

Actually, matter is not an absolute category in the universe: it is essentially an illusion. The basic elements of reality are information and energy. When energy is structured in a seemingly solid way, it appears to us as matter. Actually, it is still energy, more exactly stationary waves of informed energy.

Information is a basic element of the universe. Systems manifest not just the classical forces of interaction—physical, chemical, biological—but also interaction based on information, more exactly, on what David Bohm termed "in-formation." Evolutionary natural systems function through both "information" and "in-formation"—both are factors in their interaction and evolution. They react and respond to "information," and they "prehend" (to use Whitehead's term) "in-formation." When we complete our theories of systems with these elements, we reach evolutionary systems theory. In this theory evolutionary natural systems are formed by interaction with one another, and are "in-formed" by the cosmic matrix I call Akasha.

GS: Would you agree that the evolution of your thinking follows a trajectory that originated with Systems Theory and has now reached the Akasha Paradigm?

EL: There were various phases in the development of my thinking. To begin with, I was deeply impressed by Whitehead's "organic metaphysics" based on the concept that all things are related to all other things. These relations are not superficial, "external" conveyed merely by mechanical cause and effect. They are "internal" or "intrinsic": each thing is what it is because of, and through, its relations with other things. Indeed, with *all* other things. In that sense the whole world is a vast organism of internally interrelated elements, and all functioning in coordination and harmony.

I then realized that not only is the "whole" an integral unity but also its parts are that. There is something closely analogous in the way things evolve in the reaches of cosmic space, and how they evolve on this planet—between the physical and the biological modes of evolution. The things that undergo evolution cannot be fundamentally different kinds of things. While I was at Yale I was introduced to the works of Ludwig von Bertalanffy.I realized then that the evolving things (I called them "coagula" until then, things that coagulate the many flow-processes that make up their parts) that these things can be, and are best, called "systems."

Von Bertalanffy showed that "systems" have a similar dynamic in all areas of experience and at all levels of complexity. We find something in common when we examine all these areas and levels. They can all be described by a single theory that embraces the general aspects of all systems, the elements and processes they have in common. Von Bertalanffy called this the general theory of systems (in German, "Allgemeine Systemlehre"). This was translated into English as "general system theory," which is ambiguous. It can be read as "general-system theory" or as "general system-theory." The latter is correct. There is no such thing as a "general system." What Bertalanffy meant was a "general theory" of systems.

I then realized that these general aspects of the many kinds of systems on the diverse levels of complexity also apply to the way the systems develop. They scale the rungs of complexity from atoms and molecules, to crystals and cells, to single-celled and then multicellular organisms, and they do so according to some basic processes that hold true as we ascend from one level to the next. These are the "invariances" in the evolution of the systems, and they appear in various "transformations." But the transformations are just that: they are transformations of the invariances (just as the shape of a circle is invariant with respect to all rotations, and a square is invariant with respect to rotations of 90 degrees). In this sense there is also a theory of evolution that remains invariant across its transformation when applied to physical, biological, ecological, and social-cultural systems. This is then the general theory of evolution.

Before long I found the key concept for GET (general evolution theory) in the "dissipative systems" theory of Ilya Prigogine. I met Prigogine himself, and we developed the kind of friendship I had with von Bertalanffy. They were the scientists who worked out the concepts and the theories that I then assembled into the general framework of the laws and regularities of the evolution of natural systems in time and space.I progressed from "systems philosophy" based on von Bertalanffy's general theory of systems, to "general evolution theory" making use of Prigogine's theories and equations of developmental transformations in systems.

The next realization was that natural systems cannot evolve in the real world unless they are constantly and intrinsically interrelated. How are such interrelations possible in the observed universe? How do atoms and molecules, cells and organisms, and entire ecologies and webs of life evolve, more exactly, co-evolve? The interconnections need to be constant and multidimensional, and they must be fast; faster, I realized than the theories of conventional physical or biological signal-transmission allow.

I was looking for instant interconnections among real-world systems, and I found not one or two here and there, but an entire plethora in almost every field of investigation. Of course, the evidence is not always direct, observational; sometimes it is indirect, statistical. The latter kind of evidence is based on the fact that things could not have evolved the way they did unless such connections existed between their parts, and between them and the systems that make up their environment. Here the concept suggested by novelist Arthur Koestler proved to be relevant: the systems that co-evolve in space and time are "holons." They are "Janus-faced" entities: wholes in regard to their parts (looking inward), and parts in regard to the wholes that make up their environment (looking outward).

Evidently, I needed to find the basic concept that could explain such interconnection in nature. I found it in the quantum-physical theory of "entanglement." This means instant, multidimensional connection that does more than connect things through ordinary cause and effect. Entanglement means intrinsic interconnection: through entanglement each thing, as Whitehead said, is what it is because of, and through, its connection to other things.

This kind of "nonlocal" connection became the cornerstone of the explorations that brought me first to the hypothesis of the psi field and then to the quantum/vacuum interaction field—and finally to the Akashic field.

It was years later that I realized that the concept of this field has been anticipated in an astonishingly clear way thousands of years ago in Hindu cosmology. It was regarded as the fundamental dimension of the cosmos, the Akasha. I embraced that concept, in recognition that it was present in human speculation about the nature of reality for thousand of years. I considered it a confirmation of the validity of my concept, a significant coincidence of perennial intuitive insight with theory based on current discoveries in the sciences.

GS: You mentioned that real-world things are both informed and in-formed. What is the source of their "in-formation"?

EL: It is the Akasha. Evolutionary natural systems "prehend" (to use Whitehead's term) this deep, and in the pragmatic context of everyday perception, "veiled," dimension of the universe. This is the same as in Whitehead's organic metaphysics "actual entities" (his term for the things that appear and evolve throughout space and time) prehend other actual entities, and also prehend "eternal objects": the unchanging forms or ideas coded into the very nature of the universe. In my view evolving natural systems are shaped by their interaction with other evolving natural systems, and are "formed" that is, "in-formed"—by their interaction with the Akasha, the unseen but effective "software" that governs all interactions in the universe.

GS: In recent years, the theory of the Big Bang has been challenged by multi-cyclic cosmologies that look at the origins of the universe as a transition between cycles, making the single-shot Bang into a repeating Bounce. Thinking about Big Bounces, I had an idea that this trans-cyclic "bouncing" could be a kind of cosmic reincarnation. The idea of human reincarnation, where past-life experiences are believed to be accumulated and carried over between individual life cycles, seems analogous to the cosmic Bounces: as above so below. Do you think that the successive universes transfer information into each new cosmic cycle?

EL: I believe they do. Of course, this is speculative, yet there is meaningful evidence for it. The fact is that our universe is amazingly tuned to bring forth complex systems persisting in the physically improbable state from thermodynamic equilibrium. If this is not a fantastic level of serendipity, then either our universe was "tuned" for life right at the beginning, or its fine-tuning is the result of an act of design. The latter cannot be excluded, but it exceeds the scope of science. Within science we need to come up with a "natural" explanation, rooted in the reality of the universe itself, or, in this case, of the reality of the multicyclic "megaverse." Because the logical explanation for science is that our universe was not born with a clean slate. It "inherited" its fine-tuning from a prior universe, that is, a prior cycle of the megaverse.

This would be a transcyclic, truly cosmic evolutionary process. Each universe creates complex systems and is formed by interaction with these systems. Its tuning with complex systems renders each universe more capable than its predecessor to bring forth complex systems. This is like the genetic information accumulated across countless generations in a given species. The information is transferred to the fertilized egg, the zygote, and this creates the basis for an offspring that has the accumulated information coded into its own genetic constitution. The same way, our universe is likely to have had the accumulated information of prior universes right at the start, in the Big Bang. In that case the Big Bang is a Big Bounce. A fully "informed" bounce, giving rise to a universe that can bring forth complex systems.

Because of the transfer of information from universe to universe, there is indeed a remarkable analogy with the idea of human reincarnation.

GS: Is it the Akasha that holds all this information? Does the Akasha have infinite memory? An infinite capacity for recording, storing, and conveying information?

EL: The concept I just outlined—a series of universes that transfers information and makes each universe successively more tuned for life—suggests this. We need to add what it is in the megaverse that conveys the information from cycle to cycle. Here the current physical cosmologies give a definite and univocal answer: it is what they call the "quantum vacuum." Now we know that "vacuum" is not the right term: The enduring substratum of the cyclic universes is not empty space but filled space: a plenum. This plenum is what connects the successive universes, for it does not disappear as a universe collapses. It is the ground, the matrix, for the evolution of the successive cycles of the megaverse.

The cosmic plenum contains both energy and information, and this informed-energy substratum is not wiped clean in the transition between cycles. The megaverse is not "re-programmed" at these phase-changes, but evolves as an informed whole, toward higher and higher levels of coherence and complexity.

This is the idea that the Hindu seers, the *rishis*, came up with thousands of years ago and called the Akasha. The quantum vacuum is an information-filled cosmic plenum; we name in recognition of the insight of the Hindu seers "the Akasha."

Now about the question of infinite memory capacity. We cannot speak about anything that's infinite in the real world because we cannot conceive of what an 'infinite' real thing would be (the mathematical concept of infinity is different: that's our own creation, with properties we ourselves attribute to it, so we can have mathematical infinities, even entire series and hierarchies of infinities). It is plausible, however, that the capacity of the Akasha is quasi infinite—infinite for all practical purposes. This follows from the consideration that the most likely form of information storage in a field is the holographic form; with wave-interference patterns superimposed one on the other and creating higher-order patterns. Information stored by wave-interference superposition is extremely efficient.

It is said that a holographic medium the size of a cube of sugar coded as a multiplex hologram could contain enough information to record every letter in every word in every volume of the U.S. Library of Congress. If you think of a multiplex hologram the size of the universe (which, though unbounded, is believed to be finite), then its memory-capacity would be truly of an unimaginable dimension: sufficient to record and store the trace of all that happened in the megaverse from the initial Alpha universe to the ultimate Omega universe.

GS: Does the Akasha Paradigm answer all the questions that had puzzled you all these years?

EL: The Akasha is a paradigm, not a particular theory. It is the basis for particular theories, and the questions I have had all these years require answers in terms of theories. But these theories, if they are to be sound, presuppose a sound basis. The Akasha furnishes that basis. So I say that the Akasha paradigm gives me a basis for searching for answers to the questions that have been puzzling me. Finding those answers calls for research, not just by me, but collaboratively by everyone who is truly committed to finding the answers.

GS: While you were working on this book, were you experiencing sudden new insights, was your thinking taking on new turns?

EL: This is a book that I have been writing and re-writing. Each re-write was based on an insight that was partly critical and partly creative. It told me that what I had in the previous draft was not quite right; it had flaws. But as I progressed with the re-write further insights would appear—they would "fall in" as the German word *Einfall* suggests. I would then try to spell it out. This happened dozens of times while I was working on this manuscript.

GS: Just a few days ago when you sent the manuscript to the publisher, you told me that you had "completed your task." What did you mean by that? Do you feel that you had a calling, something urging you to write?

EL: I meant it more modestly than that. I accepted as my task to try to formulate the basic insight of this book: the idea that all the things we encounter in our experience have a common root. This root not only grounds them, but also connects them and enables them to evolve together. This has been an unceasing intuition for me over the years, and it has prompted me to write nearly a dozen full-length books on this topic and many articles and "blogs."

When I sent this book's manuscript to the publisher I had a feeling that I had fulfilled my task—for now.

I have spelled out the nature of the insight as well as I could, given the information at my disposal, and my ability to gather it into a meaningful and coherent whole. All this is provisional, subject to further research and insights "falling in." That could be tomorrow, or next year. I would then have another "task" before me. But that is fine with me. The meaning of the search for truth is not in finding it, but in the seeking. That is an endless, exhausting, Sisyphean labor. But it is worth undertaking it. What better way could we fill our life with meaning than to search for it?

GS: What about the myth of Indra's net and your concept of consciousness? Are they related?

EL: I thought that the concept of consciousness that I arrived at has been already anticipated in this ancient concept of Indra's Net. It is like a necklace a jewel made up of many jewels where each jewel reflects all the other jewels. This is different from having all together and interacting. They are each separate. If you take this notion and apply it to internal and external aspects and all of our brains having this internal aspect, organisms and they are all informed by the same basic dimension the Akasha that means that all consciousness is automatically informed by the same basic in-formation by the same basic reality so that we are reflecting as it were like a jewel all the other consciousnesses. Not because there is a god or a divine being imposing his or her ideas on consciousness of each person, but because all of our body and brain matter energy system is informed by the same virtual dimension—the Akasha. When we reflect on our own experiences, we introspect, then our consciousness is connected with all the other consciousnesses. Because our organisms are connected with all the other organisms, all the other matter energy systems operate on the same program. So it is a remarkably close account of the Indra's net.

GS: Your ideas are fascinating. They make me think of things like Jung's archetypes, and the feeling that when we enter into a dream we may enter into another person's dream domain, where consciousnesses meet without having the limitations of the physical body.

EL: these are all research topics. You need to develop observations and you will find an integral meaning, you find out how one thing relates to another. You are getting away from "ad hoc" assumptions and theories. Modern science has given up on the possibility of a theory of everything, a single scheme that can explain everything. This would be as Einstein, said, like reading the mind of God. But I believe that we can have the same basic scheme in some very diverse phenomena, which is an objective that science has never given up.

Oneness of the Akasha Paradigm

The Akasha is a (r)evolutionary concept with far-reaching implications. It changes our thinking about the fundamental reality of the whole world, which is key to creating a "world-shift" toward a sustainable planet, with ethical and moral human relations. Laszlo posits that "When we descend into the deep regions of our own consciousness we enter into an altered state that brings us into nonlocal communication with the mind-like aspect of the otherwise hidden but ultimately real A-dimension of the cosmos."[140] The oneness of individual consciousness with the mind-like aspect of the Akasha is the fundamental element of Ervin Laszlo's and Gyorgyi Szabo's "Oneness Declaration." In 2012 we created a concise communiqué offering guidance in this challenging transition period for humankind:

The Oneness Declaration

Sixteen Hallmarks of the New Consciousness

1. I am part of the world. The world is not outside of me, and I am not outside of the world. The world is in me, and I am in the world.

2. I am part of nature, and nature is part of me. I am what I am in my communication and communion with all living things. I am an irreducible and coherent whole with the web of life on the planet.

3. I am part of society, and society is part of me. I am what I am in my communication and communion with my fellow humans. I am an irreducible and coherent whole with the community of humans on the planet.

Gyorgyi: With the consciousness that arose in me, my life has taken on new meaning. I will never be lonely again, never feel alone. Because I am not alone and disconnected, I am an essential part of everybody and everything around me. I am one with the world, and have always been, even if with my earlier, and now discarded duality-consciousness, I did not know it.

4. I am more than a skin-and-bone material organism: my body, and its cells and organs are manifestations of what is truly me: a self-sustaining, self-evolving dynamic system arising, persisting and evolving in interaction with everything around me.

5. I am one of the highest, most evolved manifestations of the drive toward coherence and wholeness in the universe. All systems drive toward coherence and wholeness in interaction with all other systems, and my essence is this cosmic drive. It is the same essence, the same spirit that is inherent in all the things that arise and evolve in nature, whether on this planet or elsewhere in the infinite reaches of space and time.

   Gyorgyi: I evolve and I am master of my evolution. But this is not a separate, me-only evolution: it is a co-evolution with everyone and everything around me. How I evolve is part of how they evolve, and how they evolve is part of my evolution. I co-evolve with people and with all life on the planet. I co-evolve with the universe, and the universe co-evolves with me. In this wholeness

I am a small but not insignificant part—I am a master of the co-evolution of the whole planet.

6. There are no absolute boundaries and divisions in this world, only transition points where one set of relations yields prevalence to another. In me, in this self-maintaining and self-evolving coherence- and wholeness-oriented system, the relations that integrate the cells and organs of my body are prevalent. Beyond my body other relations gain prevalence: those that drive toward coherence and wholeness in society and in nature.

7. The separate identity I attach to other humans and other things is but a convenient convention that facilitates my interaction with them. My family and my community are just as much "me" as the organs of my body. My body and mind, my family and my community, are interacting and interpenetrating, variously prevalent elements in the network of relations that encompasses all things in nature and the human world.

8. The whole gamut of concepts and ideas that separates my identity, or the identity of any person or community, from the identity of other persons and communities are manifestations of this convenient but arbitrary convention. There are only gradients

distinguishing individuals from each other and from their environment and no real divisions and boundaries. There are no "others" in the world: we are all living systems and we are all part of each other.

Gyorgyi: With my wholeness-consciousness I realize that not only am I not separate from the world around me, I know that nobody is. The entire concept of separation is a false, illusory concept. When we act with that concept in mind we divide the unity of the world, segment its wholeness into bits and pieces. Our ego divides us, but our body does not follow suit—it acts in coherence with the whole Earth. I am part of the Earth, part of the larger whole that is the world in its totality—an almost invisible but real and inseparable part of it.

9. Attempting to maintain the system I know as "me" through ruthless competition with the system I know as "you" is a grave mistake: it could damage the integrity of the embracing whole that frames both your life and mine. I cannot preserve my own life and wholeness by damaging that whole, even if damaging a part of it seems to bring me short-term advantage. When I harm you, or anyone else around me, I harm myself.

10. Collaboration, not competition, is the royal road to the wholeness that hallmarks healthy systems in the world. Collaboration calls for empathy and solidarity, and ultimately for love. I do not and cannot love myself if I do not love you and others around me: we are part of the same whole and so are part of each other.

11. The idea of "self-defense" even of "national defense," needs to be rethought. Patriotism if it aims to eliminate adversaries by force, and heroism even in the well-meaning execution of that aim, are mistaken aspirations. A patriot and a hero who brandishes a sword or a gun is an enemy also to himself. Every weapon intended to hurt or kill is a danger to all. Comprehension, conciliation and forgiveness are not signs of weakness; they are signs of courage.

Gyorgyi: I am part of a community called humanity, and my country is the Earth. My immediate and real family is everybody in my community and in my country. Everything I do reflects not just on me, but on everybody in this community, whether they live next to me or far away. I reflect consciously on how I live and what I do, because everything I think and do affects all the others. Hurting anybody no matter for what reason hurts me, and healing and making anybody whole heals me and makes me whole.

12. "The good" for me and for every person in the world is not the possession and accumulation of personal wealth. Wealth, in money or in any material resource, is but a means for maintaining myself in my environment. As exclusively mine, it commandeers part of the resources that all things need to share if they are to live and to thrive. Exclusive wealth is a threat to all people in the human community. And because I am a part of this community, in the final count it is a threat also to me, and to all who hold it.

13. Beyond the sacred whole we recognize as the world in its totality, only life and its development have what philosophers call intrinsic value; all other things have merely instrumental value: value insofar as they add to or enhance intrinsic value. Material things in the world, and the energies and substances they harbor or generate, have value only if and insofar they contribute to life and wellbeing in the web of life on this Earth.

    Gyorgyi: My life, and the life of everyone in my community and my country, is the highest value, far higher than any other kind of wealth counted in money and material possessions. My possessions do not bring me pleasure or benefit if they harm others, make them unhappy, or diminish their chance for wholeness and fulfillment. The value of all things depends on what they do to my life, and since my life is part of everybody else's life, on what they do to all other people's lives.

14. Every healthy person has pleasure in giving: it is a higher pleasure than having. I am healthy and whole when I value giving over having. The true measure of my accomplishment and excellence is my readiness to give. It is not the amount of what I give that is the measure of my accomplishment and excellence, but the relation between what I give, and what my family and I need to live and to thrive.

15. A community that values giving over having is a community of healthy people, oriented toward thriving through empathy, solidarity, and love among its members. Sharing enhances the community of life, while possessing and accumulating creates demarcation, invites competition, and fuels envy. The share-society is the only true and valuable norm for all the communities of life on the planet; the have-society is typical only of modern-day humanity, and it is an aberration.

Gyorgyi: A life dedicated to hoarding and collecting what others or nature can give me is not a life worth living. The pleasure it gives is short-lived and paltry, compared to the satisfaction I feel when I can give to others something that comes genuinely from me. Only when I give do I feel myself happy and fulfilled, part of the wholeness I form in my community and my country.

16. I acknowledge my role and responsibility in evolving a planetary consciousness in me, and by example in others around me. I have been part of the aberration of human consciousness in the modern age, and now wish to become part of the evolution that overcomes the aberration and heals the wounds inflicted by it. This is my right as well as my duty, as a conscious member of a conscious species on a precious and now critically endangered planet.

    Gyorgyi: I now realize that I am an integral part of the world, a member of the human and the Earth community. I live my life, but the life I live is not only my life: it is the life of the entire human and Earth community. I live it the best way I can. This is not a choice for me; it is a duty. Even more than a duty, it is simply the way I am, a human being endowed with a consciousness of oneness and belonging.

THE DEFINITIVE THEORY OF THE AKASHIC FIELD

The latest, and most mature fruit of Laszlo's endeavors, *The Self-Actualizing Cosmos: The Akasha Revolution in Science and Human Consciousness* (2014), discusses key principles of his emerging paradigm that is the Akasha Paradigm. The book's objective is to enlarge our understanding of the cosmos and consciousness, and how the application of such enhanced knowledge can contribute to greater individual, societal and planetary well-being and prosperity. Laszlo's Akasha paradigm is characterized by simplicity in explanation, consistency in the ways it connects diverse elements of scientific knowledge and meaningfulness in regard to humankind's purpose on this planet.

A number of unexpected and critically-anomalous observations point to the necessity for a revolution in the natural sciences—a revolution that will trigger reinterpretations of science's most fundamental theories about the nature of cosmos, life and consciousness. "The paradigm emerging in science in the second decade of this century signifies a major shift in the worldview of science. It is a shift from the dominant paradigm of the twentieth century, where events and interactions were believed to take place in space and time and were considered local and separable, to a twenty-first century paradigm that recognizes that there is a deeper dimension beyond space and time and that the connection, coherence, and coevolution we observe in the manifest world are coded in the integral domain of that deeper dimension."[141]

In Laszlo's view, connection, coherence and coevolution are fundamental and integral features of our world. Another key feature is nonlocality, which explains that things that occur at one place and time also occur at other places and times; consequently our world is intrinsically nonlocal. The emerging paradigm provides a coherent explanation for the fine-tuned interaction between parts such as quanta and wholes such as macroscale entities in a coordinated fashion conveyed by an all-encompassing field—the Akashic field. Universal fields are, in themselves, invisible; but they produce observable effects and connect the phenomena in our world.

Laszlo argues that "the theory of relativity as well as quantum field theory are highly accomplished schemes for understanding the connections that appear among phenomena in space and time; the fields they postulate do not offer an adequate explanation of the nonlocality that has been observed at the supersmall scale of the quantum and is now observed at macroscopic scales as well. It appears that a further item needs to be added to the repertory of fields known to science."[142] He suggests that the "missing field" is a nonlocal interaction-generating holofield where scalar waves propagate in space at supraluminal velocities. Laszlo posits that "the scalar waves of the universal holofield interfere with the waves emanating from quanta and quanta-based systems, and the resulting phase-conjugating interference transfers information from the field to the system. Since the field is universal and transmits information in the distributed mode of holograms, and the waves of the field are scalars that propagate quasi-instantly in space, the transfer of information produces instant or quasi-instant interaction within and among quanta and quanta-based systems throughout space and time."[143]

As stated above, fields themselves are not observable; only their effects are. What drives or governs the laws and regularities that result in the manifest dynamically evolving universe? Could the spatio-temporal phenomena be a consequence of a deeper dimension of physical reality and not a fundamental reality as suggested by mainstream science? Laszlo explains that there is a domain beyond spacetime that is a matrix of all things and events that arise and evolve in space and time—the Akashic field—the ultimate real dimension of the cosmos. Hindu philosophy recognizes that the world we experience is only the manifestation of a deeper Akasha dimension, which is the true ultimate reality. Cutting-edge quantum field science is reconsidering the possibility of such an all-encompassing plenum. Laszlo deduces from various innovative thought experiments that the "Akasha harbors the geometrical relations that govern the interaction of quanta and of all things constituted of quanta in space and time. It is the seat of the fields and forces of the manifest world. The Akasha is the universal gravitational field that attracts things proportionately to their mass; it is the electromagnetic field that conveys electric and magnetic effects through space; it is the ensemble of the quantum fields that assigns probabilities to the behavior of quanta; and it is the scalar holofield that creates nonlocal interaction among quanta and configurations of quanta. The Akasha is the integration of all these elements in a unitary cosmic dimension that is beyond space and time. It is the fundamental, if in the everyday context hidden, dimension of the world."[144]

How did our universe come to be as it is now? Was it perhaps designed and if so by what or whom? The hypothesis of design by supernatural providence is a theological issue but cutting-edge scientific theories and cosmological models now offer a hypothesis that our universe could have inherited its coherence-generating properties from a prior universe. Abhay Ashtekar* and a team of astrophysicists at the Institute for Gravitational Physics and Geometry at Pennsylvania State University introduced and developed a model of loop quantum gravity cosmology. This model is capable of explaining the state of our universe prior to the "Big Bang" that gave rise to it, whereas standard models cannot provide such a preview. Ashtekar and his collaborators suggest that our universe is part of an indefinite series of universes—the multiverse—and Big Bangs and Big Crunches are phase transitions from one universe to the succeeding one. "The matter-component of the prior universe 'evaporates' in black holes and is reborn in the superfast expansion that follows the final collapse. Instead of a Big Bang leading to a Big Crunch, we have recurring Big Bounces. The theory of inheritance between successive universes (successive cycles of the multiverse) offers a more cogent explanation of the coherence of our universe than either the theory of random selection or a theological appeal to supernatural providence. Calculations based on loop quantum gravity cosmology lend the inheritance thesis significant support. It appears that in the transition between the successive cycles the parameters and other physical characteristics of the preceding cycle are not canceled but affect the next cycle."[145]

The hypothesis of the trans-cyclic nature of the cosmos posits that universes inherit information and in-formation from precursor universes. Akashic cosmology contributes further to Ashtekar's model by theorizing a multiversal process of evolution whereby each cycle of the multiverse the A-dimension *in-forms* the M-dimension such a way that the in-formed M-dimension *de-forms* the A-dimension. This cyclical process of learning furnishes evolution.

The Akasha paradigm offers a consistent and coherent scheme that bridges the manifest reality of the cosmos and the immaterial phenomena of mind and consciousness. The human experience of matter and mind are fundamentally different states of experiences. Can a material entity like our brain produce something immaterial like our consciousness? In Laszlo's view "finding a solution to the body-mind problem is indeed hard—at least when the problem is posed in light of the old paradigm. The Akasha paradigm offers a radically different framework for this problem. It suggests that brain and mind do not exist on the same plane of reality, in the same dimension of the cosmos. The brain is a part of the material plane of reality: the manifest M-dimension. Mind and consciousness, on the other hand, participate in, and essentially belong to, the deep Akasha dimension."[146] He further suggests that the neural networks of the human brain resonate with, and decode signals from, the A-dimension. The human brain selects and filters out A-dimensional information according to what is relevant to human life. Entering into an altered state of consciousness allows access to a greater range of universal information stored in the A-dimension as holographically entangled nonlocal information.

Laszlo's Akasha paradigm philosophy offers new insights into the nature of the universe, human perception, and well-being as well as the scope of human freedom, objectivity and the meaning of human endeavor to accomplish the highest value—"the Good."

According to his explanation, humans perceive A-dimensional and M-dimensional information in two different ways. M-dimensional information is perceived by bodily senses and processed by the brain's neuroaxonal network. A-dimensional information is picked up by the brain directly and is decoded by the brain's subneuronal networks. Laszlo states that "in today's crucial epoch, it is essential to recognize—literally 're-cognize'—that the information processed in the latter mode is just as real as the information conveyed in the former. When brought to conscious awareness, the subtle insights and intuitions that reach us from the A-dimension connect us with each other and with nature. Regaining our sense of oneness with each other and with nature is a fundamental precondition of creating a sustainable world for ourselves and for all life on this planet."[147]

A-dimensional information regulates and governs interaction throughout the manifest world and living organisms. The *Qi* of Chinese medicine, the *prana* of Hindu tradition, and the *life energy* of traditional Western medicine can explain species-specific A-dimension information. Laszlo posits that "Life can emerge and persist in the universe because living systems tune in to and resonate with information in the Akasha dimension. Malady and malfunction are errors in the way a living system receives and processes this information. In many cases these errors can be corrected. This has major and, in modern medicine, largely unexploited implications for the maintenance of health and the cure of disease."[148]

He says that modern medicine's use of synthetic substances and unnatural interventions is not aligned and harmonious with the healing powers of the human body and natural substances. "The information that governs healthy organic functioning is present in every living organism. When accessed, it can correct blockages, breakdowns, and malfunctions. Calling attention to this previously known but currently nearly forgotten method of natural self-healing is the principal contribution of the Akasha paradigm to modern medicine."[149]

With regard to freedom, Laszlo explains that according to the Akashic paradigm explanation, humans are part of a non-locally-interconnected universe and we interact with the M- as well as with the A-dimension thereby enjoying a great degree of freedom. No system in an interconnected world experiences absolute freedom, as that would mean existing absolutely "free from" external influences, which contradicts the concept of interconnection. In Laszlo's understanding, freedom is a matter of degree, which is determined by external and internal factors. He says that "consciousness can extend the range of our freedom. If we adopt consciously envisaged worldviews, and bring consciously envisaged goals and values to bear on our life, our freedom acquires an additional goal-oriented dimension. And if we allow not only the sensory information that connects us with the manifest world to penetrate to our consciousness but also the more subtle insights and intuitions that reach us from the A-dimension, we further extend the effective range of our freedom.

"In addition to information that originates in the external world, we can respond also to information that we ourselves generate. As conscious beings capable of abstract thinking and imagination, we can envisage events, people, and conditions without actually experiencing them. We can respond to this self-generated information the same way we respond to information from the external world. We can recall the past and envisage the future. We are not limited to the here-and-now. Not only can we react, we can also proact."[150]

Consequently, humans can act consciously and to use their freedom responsibly, by aligning their self-interest with the interest of others according to the principle that what is good for one is equally good for others, since we live in an interconnected and interacting world. The concept of coherence creates a system as a living whole. Finding coherence between one's self-interest and the collective interest doesn't stop at the individual or societal level but extends to the environment within which we live. The external parts of a living organism need to be in accordance with the coherence of its internal parts. Living organisms form a supercoherent system with their environment or biosphere. Laszlo says, "Ever more people, especially young people, are rediscovering their oneness with each other and with the world. They are rediscovering the power of love—rediscovering that love is more than the desire for sexual union, that it is a profound sense of belonging to each other and to the cosmos. This rediscovery is timely, and it is not mere fantasy: it has its roots in our holographically whole, nonlocally interconnected universe. Supercoherence is health enhancing and socially and ecologically sound. It gives rise to behaviors and aspirations that are good for us, good for others, and good for the world. It is objectively good. It is the answer to the quest for the highest value philosophers called 'The Good.'"[151]

For all of humankind, our understanding of how Laszlo's intrinsically-interconnected universe works has profound implications and consequences regarding our behavior, awareness, and ultimately our actions. In order for us to overcome humankind's local and global challenges we must make the concept of the oneness of the world a prerequisite, one that leads our understanding of all other thoughts and actions. In such a context, each individual is an intrinsic part of all humanity, which itself is an essential part of the web of life as a whole. Being and acting in a cosmically aware way, and only by so being and acting, can humans be positive agents of change towards a sustainable world, designing and applying coherent, conscious decisions. The possibilities that arise from this coherent Theory of Everything, this nonlocal, extraordinarily interconnected worldview, are what show, and actively unfold, the essential yet quasi-infinite benefit of this knowledge. In truth, this powerful change, which exists in the far reaches of space and time, yet can also arise within the local space of our bodies and conscious awareness, is what propels us forward from day to day as we live our life.

Akashic Consciousness

Laszlo co-authored with Anthony Peake* *The Immortal Mind: Science and the Continuity of Consciousness Beyond the Brain* (2014), which discusses and analyzes numerous research results concerning: near-death experiences, apparitions and after-death communication, medium-transmitted communication, electronically-transmitted communication, past life recollection, and reincarnation.

Their book also discusses the emerging concept of "deep dimension" and the role of consciousness in the cosmos. Laszlo and Peake make the claim that the experience of discarnate consciousness can be recalled from the Akasha and that the death of the physical body does not mean the death of consciousness. The implication of the realization that human consciousness is immortal "will mark a new phase in the evolution

* Anthony Peake (1954–) is a British author researches scientific evidence for life after death.

of human life on the planet. In this phase, the still dominant belief system of the Western world will be fundamentally transcended. There will be a conscious realization that mind is a basic and enduring element in the cosmos, and that our individual mind is an intrinsic part of it.

"The era of conscious immortality will change our relations to each other and to nature. We will not become saints and angels, but evolve into humans who live with the assurance of possessing an immortal mind. No longer will we live in fear of death; in the fear that our days are numbered and lead irrevocably to nothingness. We will not be prey to the desperate desire to grab all we can while we can, given that 'we only go 'round once.' We will lead a more responsible life, caring for the well-being of people and the integrity of our life-supporting environment, knowing that when our body dies we will not leave the world but only transit into another phase of our existence in it. Knowing that our consciousness is immortal will give us the self-assurance we need to experience joy in living and in contributing to a world we do not leave, but experience over and over again."[152]

The book debates the age-old question of human mortality and the (im)mortality of consciousness at the time of physical death. It investigates if there is any aspect or essential feature of human existence that survives the death of the body. The two authors review a long list of account of experiences where consciousness is not associated with a living brain function. If such a possibility of discarnate consciousness does in fact exist, can science find an explanation for it? Materialist mainstream science objects to the assumption that a conscious experience is possible when an individual's brain is clinically dead. However, after careful analysis of countless documented cases of Near-Death Experiences (NDE) findings suggest that consciousness does not always cease when the brain is dead. Laszlo and Peake say that "veridical perceptions in many cases of NDE has no standard explanation. These perceptions occur in the absence of measurable brain activity, yet they match the perceptions the subject would have had in a normal state of waking consciousness.[. . .] The significant fact about NDEs that conscious experience appears to have occurred during the time when the brain was clinically dead. This has now been sufficiently documented to be regarded as true beyond reasonable doubt."[153]

If conscious experience is possible at the near-death stage, can consciousness persist after death? Apparitions, visions and death-bed visitations have been documented throughout the ages and characterized by science as esoteric. Spiritual or religious traditions explain that what may appear in a manifest form is "spirit or soul." In Laszlo and Peake's view, it is a form of consciousness. Can the consciousness of a deceased person communicate via a third party, i.e., a medium? If so, how can one be certain that such occurrences are credible? The authors posit that "this is not to ask for absolute certainty, for in regard to empirical phenomena there is always an element of uncertainty. But if we find at least a handful of cases where the level of credibility approaches reasonable certainty, we will have obtained evidence that something anomalous is experienced that indicates what really takes place in the medium's consciousness."[154] Laszlo and Peake list and review many cases, which offer plausible evidence for mediums-transmitted information or knowledge, which the medium could not have produced on his or her own.

Electronically-transmitted communication with what appears to be deceased people and other unexplained entities has been documented for many decades, as well as the methodology to carry out controlled experiments in this area of investigation. Electronic instruments establish contact for electronic voice- and video-communication. Laszlo and Peake state that "absolute proof of authenticity cannot be achieved, and even reasonable assurance cannot be attained in every case."[155]

However, "We can say that the evidence furnished by credible forms of EVP* offers reasonable ground to assume that the consciousness of a deceased person can be contacted and engaged in communication through electronic instruments. Consciousness, it seems, can exist in a form where it gives rise to signals that electronic devices can convert into sound as well as image."[156] Laszlo confirms that he personally had such an experience, which provided sufficient verification without a doubt. He reported this experience in the *Quantum Shift in the Global Brain: How the New Scientific Reality Can Change Us and Our World* (2008).

Past-life recollection is characterized by the accessing of memories before an individual's birth. Some therapists claim

* EVP – Electronic Voice Phenomena

that they are able to take their patients back to past lives, where they can experience and re-experience another person, which could be someone they do not know in present life. Such regression sessions are carried out in altered states of consciousness and many patients have reported accessing previous lives. Today, many cutting-edge psychotherapists use regression therapies to relieve present-life trauma and psychological problems. They believe that such problems may have their root in past lives instead of the current ones.

Laszlo and Peake state that "whether living subjects had lived other lives in the past, and whether the recollections that surface in their altered states of consciousness are *bona fide* memories of those lives, is not clear. Yet the evidence is powerful in regard to a more basic fact. Whether or not the memories that surface in the consciousness of people are memories of their own previous lives or are fragments from the life of others, such memories do surface. They imply that the consciousness of a person who had once lived and is now deceased does not vanish, but can be re-experienced in the consciousness of a living person."[157]

This cycle of the rebirth of the soul in a new physical body—reincarnation—is firmly embedded in ancient and Eastern traditions. Belief is a significant factor in reincarnation-type phenomena, which occur more regularly in population who hold such beliefs. Laszlo and Peake focus on actual occurrence of past-life recollection rather than on the interpretation of the observed phenomena. Such a method to an explanation of how consciousness belonging previously to a living human, can seemingly reappear in the consciousness of another. Reincarnation-type experiences in children can be characterized by emotions and, memories and physical injuries in the form of birthmarks can be transferred from one life to another. Laszlo and Peake argue that "the coincidence of birthmarks and other bodily features in a child with the fate of a previously existing person is not necessarily assurance that that person is reincarnated in the child. It could also be that the brain and body of a child with the given birthmarks and bodily features are especially adapted to recall from its holding place in another dimension the experience of a personality with analogous birthmarks and deformities."[158]

Laszlo and Peake assert that certain cases of near-death experiences, apparitions and visions, after-death communication, medium and electronically-transmitted communication, past-life recollections and reincarnation-type experiences all share a common feature, which they identify as human consciousness. Is there a scientific theory that can back up the assumption that human consciousness is always involved? Mainstream science certainly cannot account for the persistence of consciousness. The Akasha paradigm theory incorporates cutting-edge findings in cosmology, brain research and quantum science as evidence for the acceptance of a new paradigm in which information believed to take precedence over matter and where space and time and entities are manifestations of a deeper reality. In Laszlo's explanation of the Akashic dimension consciousness is continuously present. "The Akashic A-dimension and the manifest M-dimension are not separate realities. The manifest world is the projection of geometrical relations in the A-dimension. The A-dimension is the *logos* of the M-dimension: it contains the algorithms that govern events in the world that is manifest to us, who live in it.

"The A-dimension is an integral whole. It has neither space and time, nor separate and separable things and events. It is an informational totality without internal differentiation: the unitary intelligence of the cosmos."[159] In Laszlo and Peake's view, consciousness is associated with matter-like entities in the M-dimension while also being intrinsic to the deep dimension, the A-dimension.

Laszlo and Peake state unequivocally that the brain does not produce consciousness—it *receives* and *displays* it. Numerous clinical studies support this claim. The authors also report that consciousness is not observable and that human beings experience consciousness in a fundamentally different way from their experiencing of entities and events in the manifest world. "If the manifest world is a world of observable things, and if consciousness is not an observable thing, then the logical conclusion is that consciousness is not part of the manifest world. This is logical reasoning, but there is also empirical support for it. It is the discovery of evidence that indicates that consciousness exists not only in, or in association with, the brain, but also beyond it. If consciousness were part of the manifest world, it could not exist beyond the brain: it would cease when the brain ceased to function. If consciousness persists beyond the functioning brain, it is not part of the world of functioning brains."[160]

The A-dimension is an information plenum that "in-forms" things in the M-dimension. Humans do not observe the A-dimension "in itself"; they only observe the *effects of the A-dimension manifested in the M-dimension. Laszlo and Peake suggest that if humans could experience the A-dimension in itself then it would be a cosmic domain of consciousness. They assert that* "The cosmic consciousness of the A-dimension is not limited to the human body and brain; it extends to all manifest entities. Every quantum, every atom, and every multi-atomic structure is 'in-formed' by the Akasha; the deep dimension of the cosmos. This is not a dualist conception, because the cosmos is not *both* a set of quasi-material things, *and* an immaterial domain of consciousness. The cosmos is one, and it can be experienced in two ways. We can experience it as external observers as well as introspective experiencers. For external observers the Akasha is a universal field that in-forms all things. And for a subject who introspects on his or her experience, the Akasha, the consciousness that pervades the cosmos, enters as his or her own consciousness."[161]

They further argue that human consciousness:

- is an intrinsic expression of the integral Akasha consciousness
- persists after the death of the body with which it has been associated

- is a localized form of the nonlocal consciousness
- "stores" and "saves" information and memories in the Akasha plenum
- can be accessed in altered states of consciousness, or by mediums electronic-instrument-conveyed experiences, past-life recollections and reincarnation-type experiences.

Concluding Remarks on the Immortal Mind

The central argument of this book can be summarized in the following sentences: "The totality of the information that made up the consciousness of the individual remains conserved. Dying is not the end of human existence; it is a return of the mind of the human being to the Akasha."[162] In this paradigm, after physical death, consciousness follows its own path of evolution in the Akashic plenum. "The paths in the journey of consciousness beyond death appear to diverge, but ultimately they may converge. There is a cyclic return to physical existence through reincarnation, constituting periods of testing and perfecting. But when that cycle is completed, human consciousness returns to where it came from: to the Akasha, the all-embracing consciousness that is the fundamental reality of the universe."[163]

While others throughout history have offered deep understanding and insight into these matters of mind, body and consciousness, it is important to credit Laszlo and Peake for providing a plausible and nuanced perspective that dramatically pushes the boundaries of our existing base of knowledge. They provide a lens through which scientists, philosophers and lay people can better understand and critically examine what we know about the immortal mind.

CONCLUSION

The Principal Results of Ervin Laszlo's Philosophical Work from Systems Theory to the Study of Consciousness and the Theory of a Universal Information Field

The Development of Laszlo's Systems Philosophy

Laszlo's Basic Theory and Two Principal Influences

Laszlo was clear at the very beginning of his philosophical exploration that to understand the entirety of humankind's existence one has to understand the workings of the cosmos, as the micro and the macro world are intrinsically connected. He did not believe that a general law that examines only human behavior is sufficient to provide a full comprehension of humankind and human behavior. A general law or laws must examine the cosmos, which is then able to explain how each thing not only *is*, but also *becomes* in the world. He stated that the discovery of the essential dynamics of the cosmos could provide coherent understanding of humankind, society and life in general. Laszlo claims that there are still cosmic laws to be discovered that can fully explain human life and behavior, and consequently societal processes. Cosmos and humankind share a common "essentiality," which is linked to the notion of general evolution.

Laszlo asserts that life as a whole is the consequence of an organization of organisms, whose particles are made of a universal substance. An inherent, interactive and dynamic process leads to either the development of a higher organic level or a form of dissolution such as death. He considers the mind a functional organic entity that shares the same cosmic evolutionary processes as an organism, yet the mind is not generated by it. Mind, in Laszlo's understanding, is an emergent entity in evolution that interacts within the organism for a coherent adaptation and selection of the organic structure with regard to its external environment. This understanding has remained a constant in Laszlo's philosophy throughout the years; cutting-edge science has only been able to provide a scientific explanation for it fifty years after Laszlo's first formulation of this thought.

Alfred North Whitehead's organic metaphysics provided Laszlo with general principles for the relationship between individual organisms and their environments. Whiteheadian thinking, which explains the whole cosmos as an organic unity of its elements wherein organic connections link every actual entity with all others, corresponds with Laszlo's understanding. Whiteheads's notion of the "actual togetherness" of entities characterized by *prehension*—the concrete facts of relatedness—greatly influenced Laszlo's thinking. Whitehead also asserted that reality is an integrative evolutionary process. Whitehead's philosophy of organism—process theology—describes the universe as one and God as not concrete but the basis for concrete actuality. Everything exists and all actions disappear and yet live for evermore.

Whitehead's seemingly religiously influenced ideas are very similar to Eastern philosophical tenets such as those in Hinduism and Daoism, and there seems no doubt that Whitehead influenced Laszlo's decision to delve further into these ancient traditions. Throughout his philosophical trajectory, Laszlo rarely uses the term "God" to denote the universal creator as Whitehead does, preferring to describe it in terms of the cosmic-consciousness of the Akasha Paradigm. Whitehead objected to the assumption that each object has a simple spatial and temporal position. His view that everything is everywhere at all times corresponds to the nonlocal concept of the universe, which Laszlo uses as a strong underpinning to his own philosophy.

We can summarize Whitehead's influence on Laszlo's philosophy in three ideas:

- in the cosmos all things interact with each other,
- all things co-evolve and make each other what they are, and
- "actual entities" are nonlocally present throughout space and time.

Whitehead supported a conception of space manifesting *prehensive* unification, whereby separate things can indeed be together in space and in time even if they are not concurrent. Laszlo's Akasha paradigm explains Whitehead's conception coherently.

For Laszlo, Ludwig von Bertalanffy's General Systems Theory clarified the relations between systems and their environments. Laszlo understood from von Bertalanffy that systems are similarly dynamic at all levels of complexity. Bertalanffy aimed to integrate the field of biology into an overall theory that would apply to other disciplines in natural science as well as to human and social sciences. In his view, systems have isomorphic characteristics and appear as such in the human world. Laszlo had not used the terminology "system" as a description for the basic entity of the world until he studied and worked with von Bertalanffy. Their collaborative efforts resulted in a concept they called "systems philosophy," which Laszlo further elaborated on his own in the coming years and decades. Von Bertalanffy provided Laszlo's philosophical development with a tool he was looking for—the General Systems Theory. Bertalanffy's isomorphic systems concept describes a quasi-universal phenomenon but, in Laszlo's view, it lacked an explanation for the process of evolution. Laszlo wanted to identify the nature and meaning of evolving entities in an organically integral universe and come to a fundamental understanding of the relation between systems and environments, in terms of what processes drive irreversible evolution in the biosphere and in the universe as a whole.

The Application of the Systems Concept to the Problems of World Order

The Practical Application of Laszlo's Systems Philosophy and the Further Evolution of His Basic Theory

Building on the concept of General Systems Theory, Laszlo used the language of systems philosophy to describe societal order, its dysfunctional character and to provide possible world system models to overcome problems on a local and global scale. Laszlo proved in his work of *Goals for Mankind: A Report to the Club of Rome* (1977) that systems philosophy is not just a theoretical concept, but is capable of evaluating and assessing value systems, cultural differences, political and economical practices, national and regional short- and long-term goals whilst also providing tangible solutions to overcome the inner limitations of humankind. His epistemological study, which blends philosophical, sociological and scientific concepts on the nature of humanity in light of current worldwide problems, was presented within a framework that sees the planet and humankind as complex open systems exposed to both external and internal change. At this stage, Laszlo emerged as a humanist and futurist as well as a philosopher scientist. His reasoned philosophical questioning and quest for scientific evidence was joined to an unwavering belief in humankind's capacity to individual betterment and his clear foresight and the vision of the co-creation of a sustainable global civilization.

The maturation of Laszlo's systems philosophy was greatly advanced by Ilya Prigogine's nonlinearly bifurcating dissipative system theory. Prigogine's concept focused on how a system would react to external changes and influences, but it did not seek to predict changes in a system with regard to interactions between internal elements. Laszlo incorporated important elements of Prigogine's work into his own in order to predict societal changes and their possible outcomes. Whitehead and Bertalanffy's work with regard to the principles and clarification of the relation between systems and their environments influenced Laszlo to concentrate on the informational feedback loop between the external and internal elements of systems. Laszlo understood that the universe is a highly coherent system encoded by complex information, which is the basis for coherence in any system. Society, in Laszlo's understanding, is a highly complex system, whose stability and maintenance depends on internal and external information fluctuations.

The characteristics of information exchange between macro- and micro-structures, and macro and micro-events determine the direction of progress—evolution. The actions of humankind affect the biosphere and, in turn humanity as a whole. Laszlo emphasizes the significance of individual action, which as a micro-fluctuation can greatly influence and affect macro-level structural change.

The Development of Unified Information Field Theory: the Psi-Field, the QVI Field, and the Akashic Field

Laszlo's Mature Concept of the Akasha Paradigm

For Laszlo, natural systems in the world can only evolve by being constantly and intrinsically-interrelated with each other by signal-transmission that is faster than conventional scientific theories can explain. The quantum physics concept of non-local "entanglement" provided Laszlo with the explanation of multidimensional instant interconnection. This motivated him to formulate his psi-field, and thus to arrive at the concept of a deep dimension in the cosmos: the Akasha dimension. His earlier works provided a foundation for the formulation of his Akashic Paradigm, based on David Bohm's theory of implicate order, cutting-edge consciousness studies, quantum physics and various Eastern traditions. The Akashic Paradigm is highly relevant today, being applicable to current worldwide sociological, economical and ecological problems. He gathered evidence to demonstrate that systems in the world are intrinsically interconnected and argues that connections and correlations in the physical and life sciences as well as in consciousness research share the same origin, which is the subtle, all-encompassing, and entirely fundamental information field.

For Laszlo, the current scientific theories do not provide sufficient answers to explain a wide range of anomalies that have come, and are still coming to light in various disciplines.

His aim is to establish a cross-disciplinary theory to provide a coherent explanation for how "things" *are* and how "things" are *becoming*. In his view, there must exist an interdisciplinary theory that bridges metaphysics, and the natural and life sciences and also religion and spirituality: an interdisciplinary theory that can account for order, meaning and evolutionary processes in the universe.

David Bohm proposed a transdisciplinary concept that explains two distinct levels of reality. Everything that occurs in the manifest "explicate order" is the expression of a deeper "implicate realm." Bohm allowed great significance to the undivided wholeness of the universe whereby nothing is fundamentally independent or separate. While Laszlo was in agreement with Bohm's theory of "implicate/explicate order," he disagreed with Bohm's notion of evolution. Bohm maintained that the manifest explicate order arises from the implicate order but did not explain the origin of this order. Laszlo claims that Bohm's universe does not evolve, but only subsists whereas Laszlo attributes a dominant role to the evolutionary processes of all systems. Bohm's implicate order is Laszlo's psi-field, later termed the Akashic field. According to Laszlo, this psi-field could be the solution for transdisciplinary unification. It has holographic characteristics such as infinite information storage and self-renewing capabilities that continually adapt to the evolution of complexity. The psi-field provides for a "unified science," which helps us to a coherent understanding of humankind, and can contribute to establishing a more harmonious existence with one another and the environment.

Science is subject to change and the enterprise of science advances through paradigm-shifts. Laszlo reckons that humankind is at the brink of another paradigm-shift and understands how much science with its achievements and shortcomings impacts human lives. Thomas S. Kuhn* pointed out that "in the evolution of science new knowledge would replace ignorance rather than replace knowledge of another and incompatible sort."[164] Misconception of the nature of the world and the nature of humanity could lead humankind to devolution. Therefore it is vital to formulate and establish a coherent scientific worldview, an all-embracing vision of the emerging world, which advances human lives in a consciously-directed evolution.

Laszlo's coherent scientific worldview describes a universe in which an all-encompassing energy sea connects all phenomena. This underlying energy plenum acts as an infinite memory-field, retaining and transferring the information of prior universes and everything that has ever happened including all traces of human mental and physical activity. Laszlo postulates that in this dense energy field, matter and mind co-evolve and living organisms are not accidental products. His view of the cosmos describes a subtle interconnectedness with all things visible and invisible in the universe. Understanding this can help overcome human beings' sense of alienation from one another, from our planet and from the cosmos, which in Laszlo's view, is the root of many of our problems.

---

* Thomas Samuel Kuhn (1922–1996) was an American historian and philosopher of science.

Human activities and their incessant and growing demands in every sphere of life are gradually exceeding the planet's finite resources, resulting in biological life-supporting systems being progressively impaired. Earth is a complex system open to energy and closed to matter. Energy enters the biosphere from the Sun, but matter, considered as energy stored on the planet cannot leave. Humankind uses the finite energy stored here but does not sufficiently use incoming energy. Humans use up more matter and more energy than they replenish and they do not use vital resources effectively while demand for energy and material resources grows globally and exponentially. Such process is not sustainable. This problem calls for new ways of thinking and understanding the world as an interconnected whole.

New ways of thinking, Laszlo says, require new values, new ethics and new modes of life, on both societal and individual levels. Thinking globally entails taking responsible decisions for the benefit and the greater good of all with respect to the environment. Laszlo insists that humankind is close to a critical tipping point. Such critical tipping points, or bifurcation points, have occurred throughout human history. Many civilizations and cultures, for example, the Babylonians, the Mayans, and the Easter Islanders, vanished from the historical record but others were able to meet their challenges by transforming for survival. Laszlo points out that our future is in our hands and humanity must consciously create a sustainable global civilization, for if we fail to do so global crises which put humanity's survival at risk are inevitable.

According to Laszlo, it is not "utopian" to build unity within cultural and religious diversity. This calls for exercise of mutual tolerance and the establishment of mutually beneficial modes of cooperation in order to create a culture of coexistence based on participatory and harmonious relationships. Humanity can and must consciously guide its own evolution. This means shifting away from egotistic behavior towards all-inclusive humanistic-, nature-, planet-centered modes of action. In order to achieve global-scale social, economic, and ecological transformation, the human community needs to transform itself, which can only be achieved by conscious evolution guided by an evolved consciousness. Laszlo foresees that by understanding the full spectrum of the new scientific worldview and the new insights emerging in science, people will look at themselves and the world around them differently and will begin to act differently.

In Laszlo's view a "holos" civilization is emerging globally whole but locally diverse. Millions of "cultural creative" act and think according to global ethics. They are consciously changing their own consciousness, and thereby acting as pillars of the holos civilization. The currently dominant consciousness is the root cause of individual and global problems; hence the evolution of consciousness is the only way towards holos-consciousness. Laszlo strongly believes and constantly reaffirms that a change of consciousness starts at the individual, "grass-roots" level, and then spreads through communities, cultures and governments to reach the global scale. Human evolution calls for conscious guidance by an evolved human consciousness.

Laszlo's notion of holos civilization rests on the existence of a holofield, the Akashic field that is the 5th field, which takes precedence over the fields already recognized by classical science: the gravitational, the electromagnetic, and the strong and weak nuclear fields. The holofield is a quantum energy field, which manifests subtle yet universal effects. Although it is termed a "field," Laszlo conceives of the Akasha as a matrix, a fundamental and multi-faceted dimension, a unified background *of* and *for* all phenomena. The Akasha is a unifying world-concept, where in-formation by the Akashic dimension and information within space and time are the crucial factors.

Laszlo's integral vision of the Akasha serves as an integral theory of everything. It offers a coherent theory of the origins of the universe; why and how things *are* and are *becoming* in the interconnecting, information-conveying and conserving plenum that underlies the manifest world.

Laszlo's information field concept, the Theory of the Akashic Field, ties together the diverse phenomena of the world. It offers connective ties between science and the ancient intuition of the oneness of the cosmos. The Akasha in-forms everything with everything else. It is responsible for the emergence and evolution of life, stars and galaxies in the universe. It is also responsible for the fine-tuned interconnections that provides overall coherence and correlation within and between organisms and the environment.

Laszlo argues that the Big Bang theory cannot sufficiently explain the origin and destiny of our universe. Bangs, or reoccurring explosions, account for matter in the universe being condensed through gravitational attraction into galactic structures. He outlines a "Metaverse" cosmology, which holds that holographic memory traces of precursor universes are stored in the Metaverse and passed on to successive universes via "Bangs" with each successive universe evolving more efficiently than it would if emerging from a 'blank slate' condition. Consequently the Metaverse becomes more and more informed and informing.

The unobservable Akashic dimension harbors the trans-cyclic process, which appears as evolution-devolution in the manifest dimension. The information traces of each evolution-devolution cycle are accumulated and stored in the Akashic dimension, so that successive cycles become more and more informed. Laszlo does not believe in the accidental occurrence of a fine-tuned universe. In his understanding, the origins of the universe-generating process is a "Metaversal Design," a design *for* evolution. According to Laszlo, the evolution of the universe has a definite direction, which is to expand in terms of structure and complexity.

In Laszlo's Akasha paradigm our world is not just things moving in space and time; that is only the surface. Below, there is an interconnected, holographically "in-formed" and fundamentally whole world where all things interpenetrate all other things. Our universe is an all-pervasive consciousness that expresses itself in space and time, creating patterns of matter-energy on all scales from the quantic to the cosmic.

Consciousness is as fundamental as energy; the cosmos is psychophysical, characterized by its mental and physical aspects. Max Planck,* claimed, "I regard consciousness as fundamental. I regard matter as derivative from consciousness. We cannot get behind consciousness. Everything that we talk about, everything that we regard as existing, postulates consciousness."† Consciousness is not material, it has no mass and yet through our consciousness we experience space, time and matter. The idea that conscious experience, or consciousness itself, has evolved, and may continue to evolve, through time and history has been expressed by many philosophers, so driving periodic paradigm shifts.

Georg Wilhelm Hegel,‡ saw history as the struggle of the divine spirit for self-manifestation. He suggested that mind, spirit and consciousness form a unity, and humanity is a vehicle through which the divine spirit finds its own realization. Henri Bergson saw consciousness as the *raison d'être* for all life, and human beings as its highest evolutionary expression. Teilhard de Chardin (1881–1955), a brilliant successor to Bergson, explained that consciousness endeavors in the course of evolution to achieve ever-greater freedom of expression through increasingly complex supporting structures such as the human nervous system. William James carried out some pioneering work a hundred years ago in the analysis of mystical and

---

* Max Planck (1858–1947) was a German theoretical physicist. He received the Nobel Prize in Physics for his major contributions to quantum theory.

† Quoted in *The Observer* 25 January 1931.

‡ Wilhelm Friedrich Hegel (1770–1831) was a German philosopher. He played a major role in Continental philosophy.

spiritual experiences in *The Varieties of Religious Experience*. In the nineteen-seventies, biologist Sir Alistair Hardy* summed up his influential philosophy in *The Spiritual Nature of Man: A Study of Contemporary Religious Experience*. He postulated the existence of realms that transcend the physical dimension as well as the usual states of human consciousness.

Laszlo's Outline of the New Science of Consciousness

Cosmic Consciousness and the Evolution of Human Consciousness

Laszlo tells us that consciousness evolves in the course of the evolution of the systems that arise in space and time. Consciousness is associated with matter-like entities in the manifest spacetime dimension, but it is intrinsic to the beyond-spacetime Akashic dimension. Empirical evidence and clinical studies support the idea that consciousness does not reside in, nor is it produced by, the brain: the brain merely receives and displays it. Consciousness is not observable and humans experience it in a fundamentally different way from the way they experience events and entities in the manifest world. Human consciousness is the expression of the Akasha consciousness; the totality of information that makes up individual consciousness is infinitely stored in the Akasha dimension. It can be accessed in altered states of consciousness, by psychic mediums, in past-life

* Alister Hardy (1896–1985) was an English marine biologist. He founded the Religious Experience Research Center.

recollection and in reincarnation-type experiences. Humans leave holographic traces of their existence in the Akasha, creating a superhologram of all people, a collective information pool of humankind. Innovative neuroscience offers cogent explanations of ways in which humans perceive such quantum-resonance information through intuitions, visions and sensations. In altered states of consciousness such as in deep prayer, meditation or hypnotic states, quantum-based information can reaches conscious awareness.

Laszlo claims that human consciousness follows an evolutionary path and progresses from ego-based towards transpersonal-based consciousness. Transpersonal consciousness is a necessary step towards the creation of a sustainable planet.

The evolution of human consciousness goes through the same cyclical phase as other systems in the universe. Human consciousness does not perish at the moment of physical death, it is immortal. The realization of the immortality of consciousness has implication concerning the way humans live their lives. It implies living without fear of death or dying, living more responsibly towards one another and the environment, and living a more fulfilled life. Laszlo's understanding of the immortality of consciousness and the role it plays in human life expands the boundaries of science's knowledge of the world.

Laszlo investigated the possibility that individual consciousness is an intrinsic part of the consciousness that constitutes the deep dimension. Could consciousness be described as the core of the cosmos? He maintains that there is observable evidence of the effect of cosmic consciousness on the manifest world. In his view, there exist a cosmic order that originates from the deep dimension, which in-forms the manifest world. He assumes that consciousness in-forms the universe for order and coherence, and does so for the universe to *be* and to *become*.

Overall coherence in the universe leads to the emergence of complex systems such as those we associate with life. Coherent multi-scale and multidimensional connections maintain complex systems and ensure their coherence with other systems in the biosphere. Without such constant and active interconnection, life and evolution would not be possible. The evolution of life points to the coherence of living organisms with their environment. The deep dimension of the cosmos is in fact consciousness that creates localized but non-localized manifestations of itself. Human consciousness could be the vehicle through which cosmic consciousness recognises itself.

An Assessment

Laszlo's Akashic Science and Philosophy, and the Evolution of Complex Systems

Laszlo's new science is more holistic than reductionist. It regards nature in terms of connections and partnership and not as objects to be mastered and exploited by humans. The Akasha paradigm, the unobservable dimension is the ultimate foundation and reality from which the observable universe emerges. Traditional cosmologies, like Hindu cosmology and

David Bohm's 'implicate-explicate' order as well as insightful theoreticians in today's world affirm the existence of a "hidden" or "deep" dimension.

The concept of the existence of a deep dimension of the cosmos has been affirmed for millennia. Greek metaphysicians affirmed a hidden dimension. Pythagoras explained an unbroken wholeness—Kosmos, Plato talked about Ideas and Forms, and Plotinus discussed "The One." Giordano Bruno claimed the existence of an infinite universe composed of an unseen substance he called aether or spiritus. Modern cutting-edge theoreticians suggest that space-time is not the ultimate reality, and that beyond there is a deeper dimension of which holographic projections are the emergent manifestations of all things in spacetime. Laszlo explained that cosmic or integral consciousness could be likened to what the Hindus called Brahman, or the Chinese philosophy calls Dao. Erwin Schrödinger argued that consciousness does not exist in a plural form and there is only one consciousness, which accords with Laszlo's view that individual consciousness is a localized form of cosmic consciousness.

What is a complex system and how does a complex system evolve in Laszlo's view? A complex system is composed of various parts that manage to maintain the system in conjunction with its environment through input processing and the production of energy, matter and information. The continued existence of systems depends on their access to, and utilization of, the correct flow of energy, matter and information.

Through these flows of energy and these processes, a complex system forms a functional unit with its environment. The unit of system-environment is a nested hierarchy of systems within systems extending to the entire biosphere. It embraces systems such as the human community, forming a functional unity with the environment making life possible on this planet and in the ecosphere.

All things that emerge in nature are natural systems and those that evolve are evolutionary natural systems. They appear as matter but are not absolute and separate entities. Matter is informed energy. Evolutionary natural systems are constantly formed and "in-formed"—using David Bohm's terminology—through interaction and evolution. The action and reaction of information result in evolutionary natural systems "prehending"—using Whitehead's terminology—each other through the processing of information.

Laszlo's evolutionary systems theory accounts for the information interaction between evolutionary natural systems and the cosmic matrix he calls Akasha. The deeper purpose behind the evolution of complex systems is the achievement of higher levels of coherence in space and time.

Throughout history, humans had a compelling need to find conceptions of the universe, a universe within which they can regard their own life as meaningful. Humans want to know how they fit into the scheme of things and how they themselves should relate to the objective world. They want to know the significance and purpose of their own existence. Laszlo's Akasha concept answers these queries coherently and offers orientation for humankind. It proposes an integral understanding of the natural and humanistic disciplines. It changes the way humans understand themselves and the world, and it helps modify human aspirations. As an integral worldview, the Akasha paradigm claims that humankind is an active participant in the integrally evolving universe and not just a passive part of it.

Humans have the privilege and responsibility to direct consciously their own evolution towards an optimally functioning society and environment. The worldwide shift towards global sustainability and wellbeing can be achieved by shifting from our current, limited human consciousness towards a more evolved, holistic consciousness. The shift of the individual's values, ethics, and consciousness to the global level is the path to survival for humans as a species.

LASZLO'S (R)EVOLUTIONARY VISION

The Paradigm of Interconnection and the Challenge of Conscious Evolution

The Akasha theory is the result of Laszlo's five decades of research and work, and the evolution of his thinking and consciousness. His multi-dimensional worldview embraces cutting-edge findings in physics, biology, and consciousness research while bridging science, religion and spirituality, with life-sustaining implications for humankind. It views humans as active agents capable of consciously directing their lives. They are intrinsically and subtly connected with one another and the cosmos. This holistic worldview encourages people to make conscious life choices for the maintenance and establishment of a high level of individual, social and ecological coherence.

There is a wide and deep trajectory in the evolution of Laszlo's thinking and understanding of the world, especially in regard to humankind's place and role in the world. He started by recognizing that the world is not constructed as separate physical, living and social things but as interrelated and coevolving things. Then he realized that if every thing is interconnected it must also communicate with all other entities. Laszlo's Akasha paradigm is a mature (r)evolutionary vision with extensibility, consistency and wide scope of application. It offers a basic set of concepts, which define the interdisciplinary paradigm of systems change, continuity and transformation in the world. His intellectual development was led by two insights: one, suggested by Albert Einstein, is that we cannot solve problems in the world today with the kind of thinking that gave rise to those same problems and the other held by Mahatma Gandhi, that we must be the change we want to see in the world.

Max Planck said that "Science cannot solve the ultimate mystery of nature. And that is because, in the last analysis, we ourselves are part of nature and therefore part of the mystery that we are trying to solve."* (*Where is Science Going?* Max Planck 1933) Laszlo tried to solve this mystery. His perspective

* Max Planck and James Vincent Murphy, *Where Is Science Going?* With a Preface by Albert Einstein. Translated and edited by James Murphy (London: Allen& Unwin, 1933).

is that of a participatory consciousness, which recognizes that there is no separation between subject and object, observer and observed, conscious and unconscious. Everything is intrinsically interconnected and coevolving.

A fine-tuned coherence of the human body, living organisms and the cosmos points to the existence of universal constants that allow the emergence and the evolution of life. Coherence between the human mind, living organisms and the cosmos points to a subtle interconnection and exchange pervading the universe. What conveys interconnection is an underlying field, the Akashic field, the matrix of the cosmic deep-dimension. The whole world is like a living organism, whose intrinsic evolutionary trend is toward wholeness and coherence, through interconnection and interaction.

Why Laszlo's Akasha Paradigm Is Fundamental in the World Today

Ervin Laszlo has been, and continues to be, dedicated to research on the Akasha paradigm and its implications for human life and well-being. His work links and interrelates scientific and philosophical theories and declarations on how humans relate to each other. The recognition that each individual is interrelated to others, nature, and cosmos is a precondition to a timely and effective shift in our world. Laszlo is considered a global leader whose strong efforts have helped to shift humankind's obsolescent world and its worldview.

Laszlo's Akasha paradigm offers a fertile ground for ongoing research and is intended to inspire and guide researchers to elaborate further our understanding of the world. Laszlo's conceptualization serves as a platform to develop, research and articulate new findings and new understandings in the fields of science, philosophy and sociology.

The further development and application of the Akasha paradigm in disciplines such as physics, cosmology, life sciences, contemporary spirituality and the study of consciousness could contribute to sustainability and a higher level of well-being in society. Laszlo's formulation of the Akasha paradigm serves as a unifying conceptual framework for many scientific disciplines while providing a bridge between science and the world's spiritual traditions. His interdisciplinary synthesis serves as a cornerstone for today's and tomorrow's scientific worldviews.

Ervin Laszlo's Akasha paradigm is a comprehensive "Integral Theory of Everything" and offers a coherent explanation of the evolution of consciousness and the conscious evolution of our species. It points the way towards a more harmonious and coherent world, with greater empathy, love, and cooperation among all strata and in all levels of society.

APPENDIX I

Biography of Ervin Laszlo

Ervin Laszlo is the author or editor of eighty-two books translated into as many as twenty-four languages, and has over four hundred articles and research papers and six volumes of piano recordings to his credit. He serves as Editor of *World Futures: The Journal of New Paradigm Research*.

Laszlo is generally recognized as the founder of systems philosophy and general evolution theory, serving as Founder-Director of the General Evolution Research Group and as Past President of the International Society for the Systems Sciences. He is the recipient of the highest degree in philosophy and human sciences of the Sorbonne, the University of Paris, as well as of the Artist Diploma of the Franz Liszt Academy of Budapest. His numerous prizes and awards include four Honorary Doctorates and the Japan Peace Prize (Goi Award) 2001. He is currently nominated (through the United Nations University of Peace) for the Nobel Peace Prize.

Ervin Laszlo's unusual career spans music, philosophy, science, futures studies, and world affairs. Born in Budapest,

Hungary in 1932, his talent for music was discovered at the age of five. At seven he was admitted to the Franz Liszt Academy under the wing of famed composer-conductor Ernst von Dohnanyi. His debut with the Budapest Philharmonic at the age of nine established him as one of the great child prodigies of the time. Following a hiatus of barely a year due to the siege of Budapest at the end of World War II, Laszlo embarked on an international music career highlighted by the Grand Prize of the International Music Competition of Geneva in 1947, and a New York recital debut a few months later. Just fifteen years old, he was hailed by New York's critics as an artist who had few peers among pianists of any age. With major write-ups in *LIFE*, *Time*, *Newsweek*, and other national and international media, Laszlo settled in New York and travelled from there to tour the five continents.

In his late teens Laszlo's childhood interest, fostered by his philosopher uncle in Budapest, in questions about meaning in nature and life and destiny in society resurfaced. It prompted him to undertake systematic readings on these fields and to follow courses and seminars in New York's Columbia University and New School for Social Research. His copious notes accompanied him on his concert tours and in 1961 were the subject of a casual dinner conversation following a recital in The Hague. His dinner partner, who showed keen interest in his ideas, took the notes and reappeared the following morning with an offer to publish them—he turned out to be the philosophy editor of the famed Dutch publishing house Martinus Nijhoff. The publication of these notes two years later marked a turning point in Laszlo's career. He was asked to join the University of Fribourg's Institute of East European Studies, and two books and numerous research papers later received an invitation to spend a year at the Philosophy Department at Yale University.

Laszlo's professional involvement in science and philosophy followed a consistent if highly personal path. His main interest centered on the perennial "great questions" of science and philosophy, in particular the origins of the cosmos, the nature and direction of the evolution of life and of consciousness, and the meaning of the changes and transformations we are witnessing today in culture and civilization. His initial 1963 book *Essential Society: An Ontological Reconstruction* was inspired by the metaphysics of Whitehead and was followed by *Beyond Scepticism and Realism*, a methodological treatise, and *Individualism, Collectivism and Political Power*, an analysis of the ideological divide in the postwar world. *La Metaphysique de Whitehead*, an application of Whitehead's "organic philosophy" to human society, served as Laszlo's thesis at the Sorbonne for the Doctorat d'Etat es-Lettres et Sciences Humaines, completing his formal credentials in the academic world.

While at Yale Laszlo read von Bertalanffy's General System Theory, met von Bertalanffy, and began to develop *Introduction to Systems Philosophy,* the seminal work with which his name became thereafter associated. Appointments at various US Universities, including the State University of New York, led to a visiting semester at Princeton's Center of International Studies.

His seminar at the Woodrow Wilson School on the systems approach to world order engaged the attention of Club of Rome founder, Aurelio Peccei, who enlisted Laszlo to complement the economic and physical "outer limits" emphasis of the Club's first Report, *The Limits to Growth*, with a human and cultural "inner limits" orientation. Laszlo's research resulted in 1977 in the publication of the voluminous *Goals for Mankind*, the third global report to the Club of Rome, as well as of the personal treatise, *The Inner Limits of Mankind*. To research these works the Executive Director of the United Nations Institute for Training and Research (UNITAR) invited Laszlo as Special Fellow; an appointment that was followed by his being placed in charge of the Institute's work on the New International Economic Order. As Programme Director Laszlo spent seven years at UN headquarters in New York, producing fifteen volumes on the New International Economic Order and another six volumes on Regional and Interregional Cooperation.

Having completed these assignments in the mid-80s, Laszlo decided to take a sabbatical period before returning to his university. He moved to his converted medieval farmhouse in Tuscany in search of the peace and freedom to analyze his experience in the academic world and at the United Nations. He returned to his quest of researching answers to the great questions of evolution in our time. His *Evolution: The Grand Synthesis* was published in 1987 and was soon translated into Italian, German, Spanish, French, Chinese, and Portuguese. It was followed by the application of his evolutionary insights to contemporary society: *The Age of Bifurcation*. Inspiring considerable debate and discussion, it appeared in Russian and Turkish in addition to all of the previous languages.

Laszlo's reading and research at his Tuscan farmhouse was soon punctuated by frequent visits to the US, Japan, China, and many parts of Europe, as the United Nations University, the newly formed European Culture Impact Research Consortium, and then Federico Mayor, the Director-General of Unesco, sought his advice and collaboration.These activities culminated in 1993, when Laszlo, one of the two plenary speakers at the Third World Congress of the World Federation of Hungarians (the other being nuclear scientist Edward Teller), proposed that Hungary, neither a major economic nor a military power but a significant force in the field of science, art, and culture, should be the host to an international Artist's and Writer's Club to complement the Club of Rome's insistence on economic and political measures with emphasis on the urgency of new thinking, better values, and a deeper sense of personal and professional responsibility. The Hungarian government responded with the offer to set up the secretariat of the worldwide organization that was to become known as the Club of Budapest.

APPENDIX II

Interview with Edgar Morin on the Evolution of Complex Systems

Edgar Morin (1921–) is an eminent French sociologist and philosopher whose transdisciplinary work integrates science, philosophy, sociology, and politics, as well as cybernetics, information theory, and systems theory. He theorized *la pensée complexe* (complex thought), a transdisciplinary way of thinking which weaves together all realms of thought and in which the word "complex" is to be understood etymologically as *complexus*, meaning "*what is woven together in an intertwined entanglement*" (*plexus*).

La Méthode, his major work comprising six volumes in total, discusses the topics of nature on nature from a physical point of view; life on life from a biological point of view; knowledge on knowledge from anthropological and societal points of view; the life of ideas, which he calls "*noologie*"; the notions of the language of philosophy and the logic of paradigm; and the concept of human identity and ethics.

Professor Morin's distinctions include: *Directeur de recherche émérite* of the *Centre national de la recherche scientifique* (CNRS), *Président du conseil scientifique* of the *Institut des sciences de la communication* of the CNRS, and President of other organisations such as the *Agence européenne pour la culture* (UNESCO), the *Association pour la pensée complexe* and the *association La Voix Du Net*. He has been awarded *honoris causa* by fourteen international universities and has authored over thirty books and hundreds of papers.

Edgar Morin is an Honorary Member of the Club of Budapest Foundation and he has worked closely with Ervin Laszlo for many decades.

GYORGYI SZABO (GS): Professor Morin, your philosophy rests upon the notion of systems theory, which explains that all objects in nature are composed of systems and interact in a specific way. You talk about system complexity and a sense of connection between the internal parts of a system and the external connection between systems. What is that particular sense or type of connection within a system and how does connection bind unity with diversity?

EDGAR MORIN (EM): It depends on the types of systems. With physical systems, the interesting phenomenon is that the association, which organizes diverse elements produces new qualities, which are emergences and which may inhibit qualities that are specific to the isolated elements. But in the living systems, and in the human and social systems of course, the connections between the parts are a lot more complex. For instance, take a human society: we find both complementary relationships, obviously, and antagonistic relationships of competition and rivalry.

The Germans say *Gemeinschaft* for "community," and *Gesellschaft* for "elements of society." I think a nation, for example, is a mix of both *Gesellschaft* and *Gemeinschaft*. When the nation is at war, *Gemeinschaft* is more important. When people from the same country meet abroad, they perceive this *Gemeinschaft* feeling much more strongly. In everyday life, different levels of relationships may interact, as a mix of the *Gemeinschaft* of the family, of the political party, of the nation, and so forth.

The problem comes from the fact that antagonism is always present, that we may try to regulate it but it never goes away.

Deep down, the problem of unity and diversity lies in their inseparability. When we acknowledge the unity of the human genre, which is a plain evidence on a genetic, physiological, anatomical, even emotional level, we can see that this unity manifests itself through differences, in individuals, in cultures, languages, etc. Unity produces diversities, and diversities, to my mind, when they isolate themselves from unity, produce nationalist or religious fanaticism, for instance.

The link between unity and diversity is inseparable, which means we must always save unity within diversity and save diversity within unity.

GS: In your view, what are the emergent qualities of a system?

EM: The emergent qualities of a system depend on the elements and organization of that system. If we look at, for example, an organization of macromolecules, which we call the "living organization," we can see it has the qualities of life, reproduction, reparation, knowledge, etc. Each system has its own emergences according to its specificities.

GS: When a system of any kind is unable or lacks the capacity to overcome its fundamental problems, it either disintegrates and regresses or it reproduces new properties and reintegrates for change to survive. Such change is a sort of metamorphosis, which is, as you said, a continuity and transformation. How would you explain the evolution of complex systems? What do you mean by this in terms of society as a complex system?

EM: In fact, when a system is unable to overcome fundamental problems, it enters a crisis. What is a crisis? It is a systemic accident, which renders the system incapable of regulating itself normally and of eliminating deviance that could disintegrate it. With a physical system, this leads to disintegration. With a human or social system, there are three possible outcomes: either a return to *status quo*—nothing changes; or a regressive solution—a lot of complexity is lost; or a progressive solution, which is the discovery, invention, or creation of a new complexity, of a new organizational factor that allows the system to transform. Nevertheless, if the crisis lasts a long time, is very brutal, then either destruction or metamorphosis is possible.

GS: Some people adhere to a worldview, which views individuals as separate from each other and the universe. Do you think that this notion of separation created our current crises in the world?

EM: It is quite obvious to me that we find ourselves in a contemporary Western civilization where weakening solidarities and communities have produced stronger individualism, which has positive sides as it allows for more autonomy, and negative aspects as individuals tend to retract over their own egoism. This is a very serious problem and I believe we really need to build more solidarity not only nationwide but worldwide, for all humanity.

In truth, everything, which is separated in the universe is at the same time non-separated. This is easily verified at the quantum level, and we can also admit it is a wider reality. Individuals in society, for example, are separated, but then they are not, they are part of a bigger whole. Individuals of a biological species such as the human species are separated, but there is continuity, a non-separation. One can't envisage separation as an absolute.

On a social level it is obvious that separation is a big danger and does a lot of damage.

GS: For many decades, you and Ervin Laszlo have been drawing attention to the dire state of our planet and our world in crisis. We face ongoing challenges in the economy, ecology, and business; and we are possibly heading towards the brink of major catastrophes. You both explained before that humans are products and producers of society. I am in society, and society is in me. Buddha and Jesus Christ introduced new ways of thinking and living. Do we need another Buddha or Jesus to change humankind's way of thinking and living in order to solve humankind's problems? What can society or an individual do to overcome local and global problems? Are there limits to humans' power of decision-making?

EM: Neither Buddha not Jesus has had analogues. Each one delivered a very crucial message and I think even today what is important in their messages should be revivified. It is quite obvious that the message of universal compassion brought by Buddha is very important and that the message of universal brotherhood given out by Buddha is just as important. But nowadays, these values have become secularized. We can advocate fraternity even if we don't believe in religion. We can believe in compassion even if we are not Buddhists; we take this message within us and we transform it.

I believe the role of eminent personalities is necessary to renew these messages according to the dangers humanity is facing today. That is the big problem! Jesus lived in the world of Palestine, Buddha in India! We are now all together in the same crazy adventure. A humanist message is necessary. Already a lot of people say so but their action is limited: people such as the Dalai Lama, Mandela in South Africa, and even Laszlo and I are trying! But obviously it would be great if someone rose, not a prophet in a religious sense but a "messenger"' someone who knew how to raise awareness amongst people to do what is needed—to save humanity.

A pessimistic point of view would say that this world is lost because there is no savior, but one can't artificially create a savior. I believe great minds will play today a universal role.

GS: Creativity of life or creation of life—which one do you believe in?

EM: I am for creativity of life. I am, because I can witness it in the way, for example, wings appeared in insects, reptiles, mammals, in the evolution of the heart, of the brain . . . The evolution of life is creative. Furthermore there is creativity in humanity. I believe this world has created itself and has self-evolved in a very mysterious way, but the notion of 'creator' is too external to this world. I think we ought to say, like Spinoza, that creativity is in nature and not that nature was created by an external architect.

GS: In your view, what is unique about Ervin Laszlo's philosophy? Do you agree with his concept of the Akasha Paradigm?

EM: From my point of view, Laszlo's philosophy has something very specific: the Akasha paradigm. I agree entirely with Ervin Laszlo's conceptions; I believe his role is very important and I help him whenever I can. The question of the Akasha paradigm remains to be studied. There is, as in David Bohm, an idea of something unspeakable, that can't even be conceptualized, that classical reason is unable to conceptualize. I believe there is in the Akasha paradigm a vision of this 'thing', which lies at the core of everything. But I would have to discuss it with him!

GS: What do you think about the evolution of complex systems? How do you understand it?

EM: The complexity of evolution comes from the fact that evolution is never linear. How does evolution happen? It starts with a creative deviation, which, if not muzzled, will develop, have disciples, become a trend. This trend may become a historical force. In other words, evolution always starts with a deviant event. Buddha and Jesus for instance were two deviants in their own societies. In fact, they had problems because they were deviant. Take Islam as well—Mahomet was a deviant—or modern science, which arose as a deviation of theology. Capitalism was born as a deviation of feudal societies; socialism is its turn . . . Complexity is that there is no linearity. Complexity advances with trial and error, risks of failure, uncertainty, and also with a lot of creativity!

Notes

1. Alfred North Whitehead, *Process & Reality: An Essay in Cosmology* (Harper & Brothers, New York, USA, 1929), 168.
2. Ilya Prigogine, *The End of Certainty: Time, Chaos and the New Laws of Nature.* (Free Press, New York, USA, 1997).
3. Ervin Laszlo, *Essential Society: An Ontological Reconstruction* (La Haye: Martinus Nijoff, 1963), vi.
4. Alfred North Whitehead, *Science and the Modern World* (New York: Mentor Books, The New Academy Library, 1925), 144.
5. Ibid., 144.
6. Alfred North Whitehead, *Process & Reality: An Essay in Cosmology* (Harper & Brothers, New York, USA, 1929), 33.
7. Alfred North Whitehead *Adventures of Ideas, A Brilliant History of Mankind's Great Thoughts.* (Mentor Books by The New Academy Library, New York, USA, 1933), 192-193.
8. Ludwig von Bertalanffy *General System Theory, Foundations, Development, Applications.* George Braziller, New York, USA, 1968.
9. Ibid., 32.
10. Ervin Laszlo, *Introduction to Systems Philosophy: Toward a New Paradigm of Contemporary Thought.* (Gordon & Breach, New York, USA, 1972), 12.
11. Ibid., 139.
12. Ibid., 190,
13. Ibid., 191.
14. Ibid., 283.
15. Ibid., 285.
16. Ibid., 287.
17. Ervin Laszlo ed., *The Relevance of General Systems Theory,* Papers Presented to Ludwig von Bertalanffy on His Seventieth Birthday, Edited by Ervin Laszlo. (George Braziller, New York, USA, 1972), 11.
18. Ibid., 126.

19. Ibid., 186.
20. Ervin Laszlo, *The Systems View of the World: The Natural Philosophy of the New Developments in the Sciences* (George Braziller, New York, USA, 1972), 6.
21. Ibid., 42-43.
22. Ibid., 52.
23. Ibid., 59.
24. Ibid., 97.
25. Ibid.,101.
26. Ibid., 103.
27. Ibid., 119.
28. Ervin Laszlo, *A Strategy for the Future* (George Braziller, New York, USA, 1974), 63.
29. Ervin Laszlo *Goals for Mankind: A Report to the Club of Rome on the New Horizons of Global Community* (E.P. Dutton, New York, USA, 1977), 1.
30. Ibid., 164.
31. Ibid., 272.
32. Ibid., 284.
33. Ibid., 367.
34. Ervin Laszlo, *The Inner Limits of Mankind: Heretical Reflections on Contemporary Values, Culture and Politics* (Pergamon Press, Oxford and New York, 1978) Preface.
35. Ibid., 103.
36 .Ibid., 422.
37. Ilya Prigogine and Isabelle Stengers. *Order Out of Chaos: Man's New Dialogue with Nature* (Bantam Books Inc., New York, USA, 1984), 95.
38. Ibid., 95.
39. Ibid., 176.
40. Ibid., 189.
41. Ibid., 313.
42. Ervin Laszlo, *Evolution: The Grand Synthesis* (Shambala Publications Inc., Boston, USA, 1987).
43. Ibid., 6.
44. Ibid., 5.
45. Ibid., 86.
46. Ibid., 91.

47. Ibid., 145.
48. IBID., 174.
49. Ibid., 109.
50. Ervin Laszlo, *The Creative Cosmos: A Unified Science of Matter, Life and Mind.* (Floris Books, Edinburgh, UK, 1993), 18.
51. Ibid., 19.
52. Ibid., 26.
53. Ibid., 34.
54. Ibid., 47.
55. Ibid., 48.
56. Ibid., 51.
57. Ibid., 52.
58. Ibid., 63.
59. Ibid., 69.
60. Ibid., 125.
61. Ibid., 203.
62. Ervin Laszlo, *The Connectivity Hypothesis, Foundations of an Integral Science of Quantum, Cosmos, Life and Consciousness* (State University of New York Press, Albany, USA, 2003), 1-2.
63. Ibid., 10.
64. Ibid., 18.
65. Ibid., 28.
66 .Ibid., 40.
67. Ibid., 53.
68. Ibid., 67.
69. Ibid., 67.
70. Ibid,, 70.
71. Ibid,, 73.
72. Ibid., 74-75.
73. Ibid., 91.
74. Ibid., 98.
75. Ibid., 109.
76. Irvin Laszlo, *The Whispering Pond: A Personal Guide to the Emerging Vision of Science* (Element Books Ltd., 1996), p.158
77. Ervin Laszlo, *Science and the Akashic Field: An Integral Theory of Everything.* (Inner Traditions, Rochester, USA, 2004), 17.

78. Ibid., 17.
79. Ibid., 25.
80. Ibid., 30-31.
81. Ibid., 31.
82. Ibid,, 34.
83. Ibid., 39
84. Ibid., 44
85. Ibid., 50
86. Ibid., 52.
87. Ibid.,105.
88. Ibid., 111.
89. Ibid., 112.
90. Ibid., 125.
91. Ibid., 125.
92. Ibid., 131.
93. Ibid., 131.
94. Ibid., 136.
95. Ibid., 139-140.
96. Ibid., 148-149.
97. Ibid., 150.
98. Ibid., 150.
99. Ibid., 153.
100. Ibid., 161.
101. Ibid., 163.
102. Ervin Laszlo, *Science and the Reenchantment of the Cosmos: The Rise of the Integral Vision of Reality* (Inner Traditions, Rochester, USA, 2006), 7.
103. Ibid., 11.
104 .Ibid., 22.
105. Ibid., 35.
106. Ibid., 60.
107. Ibid., 65.
108. Ibid., 90.
109. Ervin Laszlo, *The 3rd Millennium: The Challenge and the Vision* (Gaia Books Ltd., London, UK, 1997), 17.

110. Ibid., 27.
111. Ibid., 45.
112. Ibid., 53.
113. Ibid., 69.
114. Ibid., 86.
115. Ibid., 96.
116. Ibid., 98.
117. Ervin Laszlo, *Macroshift: Navigating the Transformation to a Sustainable World* (Berrett-Koehler Publishers Inc., San Francisco, USA, 2001), 8.
118. Ibid., 9.
119. Ibid., 11.
120. Ibid., 15.
121. Ibid., 24.
122. Ibid., 78.
123. Ibid., 103.
124. Ibid., 110.
125. Ibid., 138.
126. Ibid., 139.
127. Ibid., 211-214.
128. Ervin Laszlo, *Quantum Shift in the Global Brain: How the New Scientific Reality Can Change Us and Our World* (Inner Traditions, Rochester, USA, 2008), Preface.
129. Ibid., 15.
130. Ibid., 31.
131. Ibid., 73.
132. Ibid., 88.
133. Ibid., 125.
134. Ibid., 126.
135. Ibid., 153.
136. Ibid., 162.
137. Ibid., 164.
138. Ibid., 172.
139. Ervin Laszlo, *Akasha Paradigm in Science (R)Evolution at the Cutting Edge*, (Waterside Publications, Cardiff, California, USA, 2012), xi.
140. Ibid., 81.

141. Ervin Laszlo, *The Self-Actualizing Cosmos: The Akasha Revolution in Science and Human Consciousness* (Inner Traditions, Rochester, USA, 2014), 7.
142. Ibid., 11.
143. Ibid., 15.
144. Ibid., 29.
145. Ibid., 37.
146. Ibid., 44.
147. Ibid., 54.
148. Ibid., 57.
149. Ibid., 60.
150. Ibid., 63–64.
151. Ibid., 68.
152. Ervin Laszlo and Anthony Peake, *The Immortal Mind: Science and the Continuity of Consciousness Beyond the Brain* (Inner Traditions, Rochester, USA, 2014), 135–136.
153. Ibid., 18.
154. Ibid., 35.
155. Ibid., 71.
156. Ibid., 75.
157. Ibid., 82.
158. Ibid., 95.
159. Ibid,, 106.
160. Ibid., 110.
161. Ibid., 113.
162. Ibid., 119.
163. Ibid., 130.
164. Thomas Kuhn, *The Structure of Scientific Revolutions* (The University Chicago Press, Chicago, USA, 3rd ed., 1996), 95.

References

Aristotle. Barnes, Jonathan, ed., *Complete Works of Aristotle, Volume 1: The Revised Oxford Translation: Revised Oxford Translation v. 1., v. 2.* Princeton Universirty Press, Princeton, USA, 1984.

Ashtekar, Abhay. *100 Years of Relativity: Space-time Structure Einstein and Beyond.* World Scientific Publishing Co., Inc., NJ, USA, 2006.

Aspect, Alain, GRYNBERG Gilbert, FABRE Claude. *Introduction to Quantum Optics From the Semi-classical Approach to Qunatized Light.* Cambridge University Press, Cambridge, UK, 2010.

Aquinas, Thomas. *Summa Theologica.* Coyota Canyon Press, USA, 2010.

Aurobindo, Sri. *Powers Within.* Lotus Press, WI, USA, 1999.

Ayer, Alfred Jules. *Logical Positivism.* Free Press, New York, USA, 1966.

Bacci, Marcello. *Il mistero delle voci dell'aldilà.* Edizioni Mediterranee, Italy, 1985.

Beck, Don Edward, COWAN Christopher. *Spiral Dynamics: Mastring Values, Leadership and Change.* Balckwell Publishing, MA, USA, 1996.

Bell, John S., BELL M., ed., GOTTFRIED K., ed., VELTMAN M., ed. *John S. Bell on the Foundations of Quantum Mechanics.* World Scientific Publishing Co. Pte, Ltd., Singapore, 2001.

Bergson, Henri. *Creative Mind: An Introduction to Metaphysics.* Citadel Press, USA, 1997.

Berry, Thomas. *The Dream of the Earth.* University of California Press, CA, USA, 2002.

Bertalanffy, Ludwig von. *General System Theory, Foundations, Development, Applications.* George Braziller, New York, USA, 1968.

Bertalanffy, Ludwig von. *Robots, Men and Minds: Psychology in the Modern World.* George Braziller, New York, USA, 1967.

Bohm, David. EDWARDS Mark. *Changing Consciousness: Freeing Ourselves from the Social, Political and Environmental Crises Facing Our World.* Harper San Francisco, CA, USA, 1992.

Bohm, David. *Thought As a System.* Rutledge, London, UK 1994.

Bohm. David. *The Undivided Universe: An Ontological Interpretation of Quantum Theory.* Rutledge, London, UK 1995.

Bohm, David. *Wholeness and the Implicate Order.* Rutledge, London, UK 2002.

Bohm, David, PEAT David F. *Science, Order and Creativity.* Routledge, London, UK 2010.

Chalmers, David J. *The Conscious Mind: In Search of a Fundamental Theory.* Oxford University Press, Oxford, UK, 1998.

Chardin, Teilhard de. *The Future of Man.* Harper & Row Publishers, New York, USA, 1964.

Clausius, Rudolf. *The Second Law of Thermodynamics: Memoirs by Carnot, Clausius, and Thomson.* Nabu Press, Charleston, SC, USA, 2010.

Darwin, Charles. *The Origin of Species.* Wordsworth Editions Lts, USA, 1998.

Descartes, Rene. *Discourse on Method and Meditations on First Philosophy.* Hackett Publishing Co., Inc., Indianapolis, Indiana, USA, 1998.

Dirac, Paul. *The Principles of Quantum Mechanics.* Oxford University Press, New York, USA, 1958.

Einstein, Albert. *Relativity: The Special and the General Theory.* Routledge, London, UK, 2001.

Eisler, Riane. *The Chalice and the Blade: Our History, Our Future.* Pandora, UK, 1996.

Falk, Richard A. *Toward A Just World Order.* Westview Press, Boulder, Colorado, USA, 1982.

Forrester, Jay W. *World Dynamics.* Wright–Allen Press Inc., Cambridge, MA, USA, 1971.

Forrester, Jay W. *Principles of Systems.* Pegasus Communications, Waltham, MA, USA, 1968.

Gabor, Dennis. *Innovations: Scientific, Thechnological and Social.* Oxford University Press, New York, USA, 1976.

Gazdag, Laszlo. *Atvaltozasok az Elbatol kelertre [i.e., keletre] es nyugatra. (Transformations from the Elba to East).* Szenci Molnar Tarsasag, Hungary, 1994.

Gray, William, LASZLO Ervin, BERTALANFFY Ludwig von, GOTESKY Rubin. *Unity through Diversity: a Festschrift for Ludwig von Bertalanffy Vol. 2.* Gordon and Breach, New York, USA, 1973.

Griffin, David R. ed., *Physics and the Ultimate Significance of Time: Bohm, Prigogine and Process Philosophy.* State University of New York Press, New York, USA, 1985.

Grof Stanislav. *Healing Our Deepest Wounds: The Holotropic Paradigm Shift.* Stream of Experience Productions, Colorado, USA, 2012.

Goswami, Amit, REED Richard, GOSWAMI Maggie. *Self-Aware Universe: How Consciousness Creates the Material World.* Jeremy P. Tarcher, New York, USA, 1993.

Gyatso, Tenzin His Holiness the Dalai Lama. *Ancient Wisdom, Modern World: Ethics for the New Milelennium.* Abacus, UK, 1999.

Hanson, Norwood Russell. *Observation and Explanation: Guide to the Philosophy of Science.* Allen & Unwin, London, UK, 1972.

Hardy, Alister Sir. *Spiritual Nature of Man: Study of Contemporary Religious Experience.* Oxford University Press, USA, 1979.

Hegel, Georg Wilhelm Friedrich. *Hegel's Philosophy of Mind.* OUP Oxford, USA, 1970.

Heisenberg, Werner. *Physics and Philosophy: The Revolution in Modern Science.* Penguin Classics, London, UK, 2000.

Husserl, Edmund. *Ideas: General Introduction to Pure Phenomenology.* Routledge, New York, USA, 2012.

James, William. *Pragmatism and Other Writings.* Penguin Classics, New York, USA, 2000.

James, William. *Varieties of Religious Experince.* CreateSpace Independent Publishing Platform, North Charleston, USA, 2013.

Jung, Carl Gustave. *The Archetypes and the Collective Unconscious.* Routledge, London, UK, 1991.

Kuhn, Thomas S. *The Structure of Scientific Revoluitons.* The University Chicago Press, Chicago, USA, 3rd ed., 1996.

Laszlo, Ervin. *Essential Society: An Ontological Reconstruction*. La Haye, Martinus Nijhoff Publisher, 1963.

Laszlo, Ervin. *Beyond Scepticism and Realism: A Constructive Exploration of Husserlian and Whiteheadian Methods of Inquiry*. La Haye, Martinus Nijhoff Publisher, 1966.

Laszlo, Ervin. *System Structure and Experience, Toward a Sceintific Theory of Mind*. Gordon and Breach, New York, USA, 1969.

Laszlo, Ervin, James B. WILBUR. ed., *Human Values and the Mind of Man*. Gordon and Breach, New York, USA, 1971.

Laszlo, Ervin. *Introduction to Systems Philosophy: Toward a New Paradigm of Contemporary Thought*. Gordon & Breach, New York, USA, 1972.

Laszlo, Ervin. *The Systems View of the World: The Natural Philosophy of the New Developments in the Sciences*. George Braziller, New York, USA, 1972.

Laszlo, Ervin, ed., *The Relevance of General Systems Theory*, Papers Presented to Ludwig von Bertalanffy on His Seventieth Birthday, Edited by Ervin Laszlo. George Braziller, New York, USA, 1972.

Laszlo, Ervin. *The World System, Models, Norms, Applications*, edited by Ervin Laszlo. George Braziller, New York, USA, 1974.

Laszlo, Ervin. *A Strategy for the Future*. George Braziller, New York, USA, 1974.

Laszlo, Ervin. *Goals for Mankind: Report to the Club of Rome on the New Horizons of Global Community*. E.P. Dutton, New York, USA, 1977.

Laszlo, Ervin. *The Inner Limits of Mankind: Heretical Reflections on Contemporary Values, Culture and Politics*. Pergamon Press, Oxford and New York, 1978.

Laszlo, Ervin. *Evolution: The Grand Synthesis*. Shambala Publications Inc., Boston, USA, 1987.

Laszlo, Ervin. *The Creative Cosmos: A Unified Science of Matter, Life and Mind*. Floris Books, Edinburgh, UK, 1993.

Laszlo, Ervin. "From GUTs to GETs: Prospects for a Unified Evolution Theory," *World Futures: Journal of General Evolution*. Rutledge, Taylor and Francis Group, Philadephia, PA, USA, 1994, 42(3), 233.

Laszlo, Ervin. (1995). *The Interconnected Universe: Conceptual Foundations of Transdisciplinary Unified Theory*. World Scientific Publishing Co., London, UK, 1995.

Laszlo, Ervin. *The Systems View of the World: A Holistic Vision for our Time.* Cresskill, Hampton Press, 1996.

Laszlo, Ervin. *Whispering Pond, A Personal Guide to the Emerging Vision of Science*, Element Books Inc., Rockport, USA, 1996.

Laszlo, Ervin. *The 3rd Millennium: The Challenge and the Vision.* Gaia Books Ltd., London, UK, 1997.

Laszlo, Ervin. *Macroshift: Navigating the Transformation to a Sustainable World.* Berrett-Koehler Publishers Inc., San Francisco, USA, 2001.

Laszlo, Ervin. *You Can Change the World: The Global Citizen's Handbook for Living on Planet Earth.* SelectBooks Inc., New York, USA, 2003.

Laszlo, Ervin. *The Connectivity Hypothesis, Foundations of an Integral Science of Quantum, Cosmos, Life and Consciousness.* State University of New York Press, Albany, USA, 2003.

Laszlo, Ervin. *Science and the Akashic Field: An Integral Theory of Everything.* Inner Traditions, Rochester, USA, 2004.

Laszlo, Ervin. *Science and the Reenchantment of the Cosmos: The Rise of the Integral Vision of Reality.* Inner Traditions, Rochester, USA, 2006.

Laszlo, Ervin. *The Chaos Point, The World At the Crossroads.* Hampton Roads Publishing Company Inc., USA, 2006.

Laszlo Ervin. *The Chaos Point, The World At the Crossroads.* Piatkus, London, UK, 2010.

Laszlo Ervin. *Quantum Shift in the Global Brain: How the New Scientific Reality Can Change Us and Our World.* Inner Traditions, Rochester, USA, 2008.

Laszlo Ervin. *WorldShift 2012: Making Green Business, New Politics and Higher Consciousness Work Together.* Inner Traditions, Rochester, CA, USA, 2009.

Laszlo, Ervin. *The Akasha Paradigm: Revolution in Science, Evolution in Consciousness.* Waterside Publication, USA, 2012.

Laszlo, Ervin. *The Self-Actualizing Cosmos: The Akasha Revolution in Science and Human Consciousness.* Inner Traditions, Rochester, USA, 2014.

Laszlo, Ervin and Anthony Peake. *The Immortal Mind: Science and the Continuity of Consciousness Beyond the Brain.* Inner Traditions, Rochester, USA, 2014.

Margenau, Henry. *The Nature of Physical Reality: A Philosophy of Modern Physics*. McGraw-Hill Publisher, New York, USA, 1950.

Maxwell, James Clerk. *A Treatise on Electricity and Magnetism: Volume 1*. Cambridge University Press, UK, 2010.

Meadows, Donella H. *The Limits to Growth: A Report for the Club of Rome's Project on the Predicament of Mankind*. Macmillan, USA, 1979.

Morin, Edgar. *L'intelligence de la complexité*. Éditions L'Harmattan, Paris, France. 2000.

Morin, Edgar and Nicolas Hulot. *L'an I de l'ère écologique: La Terre dépend de l'homme qui dépend de la Terre*. Editions Tallandier, Paris, France. 2007.

Morin Edgar and Patrick Viveret. *Comment vivre en temps de crise ?* Bayard Éditions, Montrouge, France. 2010.

Morin, Edgar. *Sociologie*. Point Essais, Paris, France. 2007.

Morin, Edgar, CIURANA Emilio-Roger, MOTTA Raul. *Eduquer pour l'ère planétaire: La pensée complexe comme Méthode d'apprentissage dans l'erreur et l'incertitude humaine*. Jacob Duvernet Editions, France, 2003.

Morin, Edgar. *La complexité humaine*. Flammarion, Paris, France. 2008.

Morin, Edgar. *La Voie: Pour l'avenir de l'humanité*. Fayard/Pluriel, Paris, France, 2012.

Morin, Edgar. *La Méthode: L'Humanité de l'humanité. L'identité humaine*. Seuil, Paris, France. 2013

Morin, Edgar. *La Méthode: Ethique*. Seuil, Paris, France. 2013.

Newton, Isaac Sir. *The Principia: Mathematical Principles of Natural Philosophy*. CreateSpace Independent Publishing Platform, USA, 2013.

Northrop Frye, Herman. *Anatomy of Criticism: Four Essays*. Princeton University Press, Princeton, Usa, 1971.

Peake, Anthony. *The Labyrinth of Time: The Illusion of Past, Present and Future*. Arcturus Publishing Ltd., London, UK, 2012.

Peccei, Aurelio. *Before It Is Too Late*. Kodansha Amer Inc., USA, 1984.

Penrose, Roger, CERCIGNANI Carlo. *Ludwig Boltzmann: The Man Who Tursted Atoms*. OUP Oxford, New Ed., USA, 2006.

Planck, Max. *Where Is Science Going?* Allen & Unwin, University of Michigan, USA, 1933.

Plato. *Theaetetus.* Translated by Benjamin Jowett. Echo Library, Middlesex, UK, 2006.

Plotinus. *Essential Plotinus.* Hackett Publishing Co., Inc., Indianapolis, Indiana, USA, 1975.

Pouvreau, David, DRACK Manfred. "On the history of Ludwig von Bertalanffy's 'General Systemology,' and on Its Relationship to Cybernetics," *International Journal of General Systems*, 2007, 36(3), 281-337.

Price, Lucien. *Dialogues d'Alfred North Whitehead enregistrés par Lucien Price.* Mentor Books, The New Academy Library, New York, USA, 1946.

Prigogine, Ilya, STENGERS Isabelle. *Order Out of Chaos: Man's New Dialogue with Nature.* Bantam Books Inc., New York, USA, 1984.

Prigogine, Ilya. *The End of Certainty: Time, Chaos and the New Laws of Nature.* Free Press, New York, USA, 1997.

Prigogine, Ilya. *From Being to Becoming: Time and Complexity in the Physical Sciences.* W.H. Freeman Ltd., UK, 1980.

Ray, Paul H., ANDERSON Sherry Ruth. *The Cultural Creatives: How 50 Million People are Changing the World.* Crown Publications, USA, 2001.

Rosen, Robert. *Life Itself: A Comprehensive Inquiry into the Nature, Origin, and Fabrication of Life (Complexity in Ecological Systems).* Columbia University Press, New York, 2005.

Rouvroy, Claude Henri de, Comte de Saint-Simon. *Œuvres De Saint-Simon.* Nabu Press, Charleston, SC, USA, 2011.

Russel, Bertrand. *History of Western Philosopy.* Routledge, London, UK, 2004.

Russell, Peter. *Waking Up in Time.* Origin Press, Novato, CA, USA, 1992.

Schrodinger, Erwin. *Scape-Time Structure.* Cambridge University Press, UK, 1985.

Sheldrake, Rupert. *Presence of the Past: Morphic Resonance and the Memory of Nature.* Park Street Press, Rochester, Vermont, USA, 2012.

Smith, Robert Angus. *Memoir of John Dalton, and History of the Atomic Theory up to His Time.* Adamant Media Corporation, Boston, MA, USA, 2001.

Stapp, Henry P. *Mind, Matter and Quantum Mechanics.* Springer, New York, USA, 2009.

Stevenson, Ian. *Children Who Remember Previous Lives: A Question of Reincarnation.* McFarland Co., Inc., NC, USA, 2001.

Taylor, Alfred Edward. *Plato: The Man and His Work.* The World Publishing Company, Cleveland, Ohio, USA, 11e éd 1966.

Tesla, Nikola. *My Inventions and Other Writings.* Penguin Classics, New York USA, 2011.

Thomson, David W. III., BOURASSA Jim D. *Secrets of the Aether: Unified Force Theory, Dark Matter and Consciousness.* Aenor Trust, OR, USA, 2007.

Thomson, William, Premier Baron Kelvin. *Popular lectures and addresses, Vol., 1.* Macmillan and co., London, UK, 1891.

Trismegistus, Hermes. *The Corpus Hermeticum.* IAP, USA, 2009.

Weber, Max. *The Protestant Ethic and the Spirit of Capitalism.* Merchant Books, New York, USA, 2013

Wittgenstein, Ludwig J.J. *Remarks on Colour.* University of California Press, Oakland, CA, USA, 1978.

Whitehead, Alfred North. *Science and the Modern World.* Mentor Books, The New Academy Library, New York, USA, 1925.

Whitehead, Alfred North. *Process & Reality: An Essay in Cosmology.* Harper & Brothers, New York, USA, 1929.

Whitehead, Alfred North. *The Function of Reason.* Princeton University Press, USA, 1929.

Whitehead, Alfred North. *Adventures of Ideas, A Brilliant History of Mankind's Great Thoughts.* Mentor Books by The New Academy Library, New York, USA, 1933.

Whitehead, Alfred North. *The Aims of Education.* Mentor Books by The New Academy Library, New York, USA, 1929.

Wilber, Ken. *Integral Psycholgoy: Consciousness, Spirit, Psychology, Therpay.* Shambala Press, USA, 2000.

Woolger, Roger. *Other Lives, Other Selves: A Jungian Psychotherapist Discovers Past Lives.* Bantam Books, New York, USA, 1988.

Index

B

C

D

E

F

G

H

N

Q

R

Z

About the Author

Gyorgyi Szabo holds a PhD in sociology with a Summa Cum Laude awarded by the Sorbonne, the University of Paris; a master's degree in philosophy from Trinity St. David, University of Wales; and a bachelor's degree with honors from Birkbeck College, University of London. She is also a trained Reiki and Reconnective Healing practitioner.

She has lived in America, England, Italy, France, and Spain. She currently lives in Budapest, Hungary. Her holistic approach to metaphysics and interest in conscious evolution serves as foundation for her work in facilitating cooperative evolution toward a peaceful and sustainable world.

Gyorgyi serves as the Director of Research at the Laszlo Institute for New Paradigm Research (LI-NPR) in Italy. She is also Director of Academic Research and Dean of Doctoral Studies at Ubiquity University. She also serves as Member of the Advisory Board of the Memnosyne Foundation.

Dr. Szabo collaborated with Ervin Laszlo in preparing the annual Conferences of the World Cultural Forum in China and is a member of the Executive Committee of the Club of Budapest (the division headquartered in France). In 2012, in association with Barbara Marx Hubbard, she founded UniverSoul, www.universoul.eu a Hub for Conscious Evolution in Paris and serves as its president. Her papers and monographs have appeared inter alia in The Scientific and Medical Network Review, The Shift Network, and *World Futures: The Journal of New Paradigm Research.*